Jerry Sittser has given us all a wondrous gift—the privilege of walking with him through his horror, his incomparable loss, his fear, his confusion, his inexpressible grief, and into his discovery that, while never "getting over" the tragedy that crushed him, he was, little by little, in snippets and fragments, being redeemed through it. What a splendid gift his book is; it is tender, transparent, tough, honest, so beautifully simple, and ultimately triumphant. I felt as I read it that I was being prepared for my own time of sorrow; when it comes, I hope I shall remember to read this book again.

LEWIS SMEDES

There is no attempt here to disguise or look away from the fact that the tragedy Gerald Sittser suffered is a deep and irrevocable loss. But in how he has slowly learned to move beyond owning his loss to owning it redemptively, we see grace revealed. To all, like him, who must live with loss and beyond, this book will be a true companion. I know of none better.

NICHOLAS WOLTERSTORFF

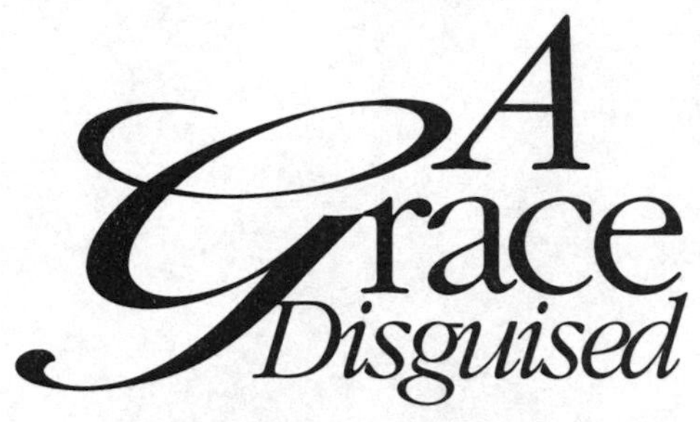

How the Soul Grows Through Loss

A Grace Disguised

How the Soul Grows Through Loss

GERALD L. SITTSER

ZondervanPublishingHouse

Grand Rapids, Michigan

A Division of HarperCollins*Publishers*

A Grace Disguised
Copyright © 1996 by Gerald L. Sittser

Requests for information should be addressed to:

ZondervanPublishingHouse
Grand Rapids, Michigan 49530

ISBN: 0-310-20230-2 (hardcover)

This edition printed on acid-free paper and meets the American National Standards Institute Z39.48 standard.

Edited by Verlyn D. Verbrugge
Interior design by Sue Vandenberg-Koppenol

Printed in the United States of America

To Diane and Jack:
blood is thicker
than water,
and faith is
thickest of all

CONTENTS

PREFACE

This book is about catastrophic loss and the transformation that can occur in our lives because of it. What I have written has grown out of my experience, but it is not exclusively about my experience. The book is like a painting that has become more than the scene that inspired it. Once I started to think about my own loss, I found myself exploring a new world of meaning that opened up before me. I began to ask questions and eventually to find answers that proved to be both satisfying and unsettling.

As I reflected on the story of my loss, which I will tell shortly, I learned that, though entirely unique (as all losses are), it is a manifestation of a universal experience. Sooner or later all people suffer loss, in little doses or big ones, suddenly or over time, privately or in public settings. Loss is as much a part of normal life as birth, for as surely as we are born into this world we suffer loss before we leave it.

It is not, therefore, the *experience* of loss that becomes the defining moment of our lives, for that is as inevitable as death, which is the last loss awaiting us all. It is how we *respond* to loss that matters. That response will largely determine the quality, the direction, and the impact of our lives.

This book is not intended to help anyone get over or even through the experience of catastrophic loss, for I believe that "recovery" from such loss is an unrealistic and even harmful expectation, if by recovery we mean resuming the way we lived and felt prior to the loss. Instead, the book is intended to show how it is possible to live in and be enlarged by loss, even as we continue to experience it. That is why I will emphasize the power of response. Response involves the *choices* we make, the *grace* we receive, and ultimately the *transformation* we experience in the loss. My aim is not to provide quick and painless solutions but to point the way to a lifelong journey of growth.

Loss is like a terminal illness. There is nothing we can do to spare ourselves from such sickness, except perhaps put it off for a while. But there is another sickness that we can heal—the sickness of our souls. In matters of the soul, I do not want to treat symptoms but to heal the illness. If we face loss squarely and respond to it wisely, we will actually become healthier people, even as we draw closer to physical death. We will find our souls healed, as they can only be healed through suffering.

Friends urged me to write this book after many long conversations. I was not inclined to write anything after my loss, though I did, for my own private reasons, keep a journal of my experience and what came of it. If anything, I recoiled from the idea of telling my story to the public. But my friends suggested that my experience was not the point. It was my *reflections* on the experience that were valuable to them, for they believed that those reflections transcended the experience and showed promise of helping others. Obviously, their opinions persuaded me.

Though I offer vignettes of my story throughout these pages, I decided to write a book about the *universal* experience of loss rather than my own particular experience alone. I wanted to use restraint about my own story for the sake of my privacy. I also wanted to guard against drawing so much attention to my story that I neglected to explore the universal issues to which all of our stories of loss point. Besides, I am not sure it is entirely possible to communicate the utterly devastating nature of one's suffering. Some experiences are so terrible that they defy description.

Still, I feel compelled to say at the outset, however inadequate my words, that what has happened to me has pressed me to the limit. I have come face to face with the darker side of life and with the weakness of my own human nature. As vulnerable as I feel most of the time, I can hardly call myself a conqueror. If I give the impression I think myself heroic, perfect, or strong, then I give the wrong impression. My experience has only confirmed in my mind how hard it is to face loss and how long it takes to grow from it. But it has also reminded me how meaningful and wonderful life can be, even and especially in suffering.

Writing this book has turned out to be meaningful but not cathartic. It has not exacerbated the trauma, nor has it helped to heal it. Keeping a journal over the past three years did that. Still, I found myself enriched by rereading my journal and reflecting on what has come out of my experience and how I have changed. This book is the product of that reflection. It is the happy result of a bad experience.

Yet writing this book has not mitigated my sense of bewilderment and sadness. The help it may bring to others does not justify the loss or explain the tragedy. My suffering is as puzzling and horrible to me now as it was the day it happened. The good that may come out of the loss does not erase its badness or excuse the wrong done. Nothing can do that.

Many people have contributed significantly to the publication of this book. The acknowledgments I make here so briefly to honor them are like an applause at the end of a brilliant performance of a Mozart opera. My praise falls so far short of the greatness of the service to which it points. These people are dear friends who have done more than read parts or all of the various drafts of the manuscript. They have invested themselves into my life. Not only what I have written but also who I am is a product of their love and concern. It is a privilege to acknowledge my indebtedness to them.

I have heard many moving stories about loss over the past three years but have decided to tell only a few of those stories here. I am grateful to Leanna, Steve, Joanne, Andy and Mary, and Jeff for their willingness to tell their stories to me and to give me permission to use them in the book. Their courage, endurance, and wisdom have helped me far more than I can express.

Linda Lawrence Hunt, Steve and Kathy Pederson, Forrest Baird, and Martin E. Marty played a special role in encouraging me to write the book. Dale and Kathy Bruner, Terry and Suzette McGonigal, Judy Palpant, and Dave Bast brought theological perspective to the book. Rachel Johnson, Glena Shubarth, and Janelle Thayer, all therapists, lent their expertise in psychology to the manuscript, while Leonard Oakland and Howard and Pat Stien added their literary sensibilities to the project. Terry Mitchell did a superb job of editing the manuscript before the book ever fell into the hands of the editors at Zondervan. Once I started working with Zondervan, Ann Spangler, Senior Acquisitions Editor, showed sensitivity to both who the author is and what the author writes. And Verlyn D. Verbrugge, Senior Editor, touched up the manuscript at just the right points.

Ron and Julie Pyle, Todd and Monica Holdridge, Dale Soden, and Steve and Richelle Mills, all close friends, assisted in shaping the ideas of the book through many long conversations. My mother-in-law, Minnie Dethmers, my sister-in-law, Judie Koerselman, and other family members on my wife's side became partners at a distance as we learned to live with circumstances that none of us wanted. My dad, Gerald, was faithful in calling and in correspondence, though he lives at a great distance. My three children, Catherine, David, and John, never once looked at the manuscript, but they played a major role in bringing vitality into my life when I most needed it. For a time I think they kept me alive; now they keep me going.

No one has contributed more to me and to the writing of this book than my sister, Diane, and my brother-in-law, Jack, who spent hundreds of hours talking with me about most of the ideas contained in this book, who read every draft of the manuscript, and who have invested so much of themselves in my children and me. It is rare and wonderful when family members are best friends. I have had that experience with Diane and Jack. I dedicate this book to them with gratitude and affection.

The End and the Beginning

You know as well as I there's more . . .
There's always one more scene no matter.

Archibald McLeish

Catastrophic loss wreaks destruction like a massive flood. It is unrelenting, unforgiving, and uncontrollable, brutally erosive to body, mind, and spirit. Sometimes loss does its damage instantly, as if it were a flood resulting from a broken dam that releases a great torrent of water, sweeping away everything in its path. Sometimes loss does its damage gradually, as if it were a flood resulting from unceasing rain that causes rivers and lakes to swell until they spill over their banks, engulfing, saturating, and destroying whatever the water touches. In either case, catastrophic loss leaves the landscape of one's life forever changed.

My experience was like a dam that broke. In one moment I was overrun by a torrent of pain I did not expect.

Lynda, my wife of nearly twenty years, loved to be around her children. Each one of them was a gift to her because, after eleven years of infertility, she never thought she would have any of her own. Though she earned a master's degree in music from the University of Southern California, became a professional singer, choir director, and voice coach, and served church and community, she could never entirely let go of her longing for children. When she delivered four healthy children in six years, she was overjoyed. She relished the wonder of motherhood.

In the fall of 1991 Lynda was teaching a unit of home school to our two oldest children, Catherine and David, on Native American culture. She decided to complete the unit of study by attending a powwow at a Native American reservation in rural Idaho. So we piled our four children into the minivan on a Friday afternoon to drive to the reservation, where we planned to have dinner with the tribe and witness our first powwow. My mother, Grace, who had come to visit us for the weekend, decided to join us on the excursion. At dinner we talked with tribal leaders about their projects and problems—especially the abuse of alcohol, which undermined so much of what they were trying to accomplish.

After dinner we strolled to a small gymnasium, where the powwow had already begun. Once again we sat with several tribal leaders, and they explained the dances that tribal members were performing and the traditional dress the dancers were wearing. One dance in particular moved me—a dance of mourning for a loved one from the tribe who had recently died. I was mesmerized by the slow, understated movement of the few who danced before us. The dance, chant, and drumbeat created a mood reflecting the sorrow that they—and now we—felt.

After about an hour of watching the powwow, several children from the tribe approached us and invited our two daughters, Catherine and Diana Jane, to join them in a dance. The boys decided to explore the gymnasium for a while. That gave Lynda and me an opportunity to learn more about the tribe.

By 8:15 P.M., however, the children had had enough. So we returned to our van, loaded and buckled up, and left for home. By then it was dark. Ten minutes into our trip home I noticed an oncoming car on a lonely stretch of highway driving extremely fast. I slowed down at a curve, but the other car did not. It jumped its lane and smashed head-on into our minivan. I learned later that the alleged driver was Native American, drunk, driving eighty-five miles per hour. He was accompanied by his pregnant wife, also drunk, who was killed in the accident.

I remember those first moments after the accident as if everything was happening in slow motion. They are frozen into my memory with a terrible vividness. After recovering my breath, I turned around to survey the damage. The scene was chaotic. I remember the look of terror on the faces of my children and the feeling of horror that swept over me when I saw the unconscious and broken bodies of Lynda, my four-year-old daughter Diana Jane, and my mother. I remember getting Catherine (then eight), David (seven), and John (two) out of the van through my door, the only one that would open. I remember taking pulses, doing mouth-to-mouth resuscitation, trying to save the dying and calm the living. I remember the feeling of panic that struck my soul as I watched Lynda, my mother, and Diana Jane all die before my eyes. I remember the pandemonium that followed—people gawking, lights flashing from emergency vehicles, a helicopter whirring overhead, cars lining up, medical experts doing what they could to help. And I remember the realization sweeping over me that I would soon plunge into a darkness from which I might never again emerge as a sane, normal, believing man.

In the hours that followed the accident, the initial shock gave way to an unspeakable agony. I felt dizzy with grief's vertigo, cut off from family and friends, tormented by the loss, nauseous from the pain. After arriving at the hospital, I paced the floor like a caged animal, only recently captured. I was so bewildered that I was unable to voice questions or think rationally. I felt wild with fear and agitation, as if I was being stalked by some deranged killer from whom I could not escape. I could not stop crying. I could not silence the deafening noise of crunching metal, screaming sirens, and wailing children. I could not rid my eyes of the vision of violence, of shattering glass and shattered bodies. All I wanted was to be dead. Only the sense of responsibility for my three surviving children and the habit of living for forty years kept me alive.

That torrent of emotion swept away the life I had cherished for so many years. In one moment my family as I had known and cherished it was obliterated. The woman to whom I had been married for two decades was dead; my beloved Diana Jane, our third born, was dead; my mother, who had given birth to me and raised me, was dead. Three generations—gone in an instant!

That initial deluge of loss slowly gave way over the next months to the steady seepage of pain that comes when grief, like floodwaters refusing to subside, finds every crack and crevice of the human spirit to enter and erode. I thought that I was going to lose my mind. I was overwhelmed with depression. The foundation of my life was close to caving in.

Life was chaotic. My children too experienced intense grief and fear. John was seriously injured; he broke his femur in the accident, which required him to be in traction for three weeks and in a body cast for another eight weeks. People from everywhere called on the telephone, sent letters, and reached out to help and mourn. Responsibilities at home and work accumulated like trash on a vacant lot, threatening to push me toward collapse. I remember sinking into my favorite chair night after night, feeling so exhausted and anguished that I wondered whether I could survive another day, whether I *wanted* to survive another day. I felt punished by simply being alive and thought death would bring welcomed relief.

I remember counting the consecutive days in which I cried. Tears came for forty days, and then they stopped, at least for a few days. I marveled at the genius of the ancient Hebrews, who set aside forty days for mourning, as if forty days were enough. I learned later how foolish I was. It was only *after* those forty days that my mourning became too deep for tears. So my tears turned to brine, to a bitter and burning sensation of loss that tears could no longer express. In the months that followed I actually longed for the time when the sorrow had been fresh and tears came easily. That emotional release would have lifted the burden, if only for a while.

Of course I had no way of anticipating the adjustments I would have to make and the suffering I would have to endure in the months and years ahead. Still, on the night of the tragedy, I was given a window of time between the accident and our arrival at the hospital that presaged, at least initially, what lay ahead for me. Because the accident occurred in rural Idaho, just outside the Indian reservation, we were at the scene for well over an hour before an emergency vehicle transported the four of us to a hospital—another hour away. Those two hours between the accident and our arrival at the hospital became the most vivid, sobering, memorable moments of reflection I have ever had or will ever have. I was lifted momentarily out of space and time as I knew it and was suspended somehow between two worlds.

One was the world of my past, so wonderful to me, which was now lying in a tangle of metal on the side of the road; the other was the world of my future, which awaited me at the end of that long ride to the hospital as a vast and frightening unknown. I realized that something incomprehensible and extraordinary had just happened. By some strange twist of fate or mysterious manifestation of divine providence I had been suddenly thrust into circumstances I had not chosen and could never have imagined. I had become the victim of a terrible tragedy. I ransacked my mind for options that would provide a way out of the pain I knew intuitively loomed ahead for me and my family. In that brief window of time I exhausted all possibilities except one. I realized that I would have to suffer and adjust; I could not avoid it or escape it. There was no way out but ahead, into the abyss. The loss brought about by the accident had changed my life, setting me on a course down which I had to journey whether I wanted to or not. I was assigned both a tremendous burden and a terrible challenge. I faced the test of my life. One phase of my life had ended; another, the most difficult, was about to begin. When the emergency vehicle arrived at the hospital, I stepped out into a whole new world.

Whose Loss Is Worse?

In the last resort it is highly improbable that there could ever be a therapy which gets rid of all difficulties. Man needs difficulties; they are necessary for health.

CARL JUNG

All people suffer loss. Being alive means suffering loss.

Sometimes the loss is natural, predictable, and even reversible. It occurs at regular intervals, like the seasons. We experience the loss, but after days or months of discomfort we recover and resume life as usual, the life that we wanted and expected. The winter's loss leads to the spring of recovery. Such losses characterize what it means to live as normal human beings. Living means changing, and change requires that we lose one thing before we gain something else.

Thus we lose our youth but gain adulthood. We lose the security of home but gain the independence of being on our own. We lose the freedom of singleness but gain the intimacy of marriage. We lose a daughter but gain a son-in-law. Life is a constant succession of losses and gains. There is continuity and even security in this process. We remember the losses that lie behind us, and we look forward to the gains that lie ahead. We live suspended between the familiar past and the expected future. The scenery we enjoy today gradually fades into the background, finally receding from sight. But what looms ahead comes nearer and gets clearer, until it becomes the scenery of the present moment that fills our vision.

But there is a different kind of loss that inevitably occurs in all of our lives, though less frequently and certainly less predictably. This kind of loss has more devastating results, and it is irreversible. Such loss includes terminal illness, disability, divorce, rape, emotional abuse, physical and sexual abuse, chronic unemployment, crushing disappointment, mental illness, and ultimately death. If normal, natural, reversible loss is like a broken limb, then catastrophic loss is like an amputation. The results are permanent, the impact incalculable, the consequences cumulative. Each new day forces one to face some new and devastating dimension of the loss. It creates a whole new context for one's life.

Stories of such loss often capture our attention, and we usually remember the most sensational ones. Many years ago my mother and I drove cross-country from Grand Rapids, Michigan, where I grew up, to vacation in Lynden, Washington, where my mother grew up and still had many relatives. Somewhere in South Dakota we stopped to fill up the car with gasoline. While waiting for the attendant to finish the job (those were the days before self-service), we got out of the car for a stretch. We immediately noticed two cars in the corner of the parking lot, both so completely smashed up that it was impossible for us to tell what model or color they were.

My mother asked the attendant what had happened. He said that on the night before, two cars loaded with teenagers had been playing chicken on some back country road. Neither driver wanted to be the chicken, so neither driver swerved. The head-on collision killed nine people; not one person survived the crash. I was a teenager at the time. Their foolishness left a deep impression on me I will never forget. I walked over to the cars and peered inside, surveying what had become a chamber of death for those nine people. I wondered why they had done such a foolish thing and how their families and friends would face the terrible loss. I shivered with fear in the face of that tragedy. I had never witnessed an accident so severe and brutal.

We tend to quantify and compare suffering and loss. We talk about the numbers killed, the length of time spent in the hospital, the severity of abuse, the degree of family dysfunction, the difficulty and inconvenience of illness, the complexity of details during a divorce, or the strings of bad luck. I have done so myself. After the accident I found myself for the first time on the receiving end of this process. The newspapers covered the story for several days running. I received hundreds of telephone calls, thousands of cards and letters. I became an instant celebrity—someone whose loss could not be imagined or surpassed. Consequently, I often heard comments like, "Three generations killed in one accident!" Or, "All the important women in your life gone, except for poor Catherine!" And most frequently, "I know people who have suffered, but nothing compared to you. Yours is the worst loss I have ever heard about."

But I question whether experiences of such severe loss can be quantified and compared. Loss is loss, whatever the circumstances. All losses are bad, only bad in different ways. No two losses are ever the same. Each loss stands on its own and inflicts a unique kind of pain. What makes each loss so catastrophic is its devastating, cumulative, and irreversible nature.

What value is there to quantifying and comparing losses? My own loss was sudden and traumatic, as if an atomic blast went off, leaving the landscape of my life a wasteland. Likewise, my suffering was immediate and intense, and I plunged into it as if I had fallen over a cliff. Still, the consequences of the tragedy were clear. It was obvious what had happened and what I was up against. I could therefore quickly plot a course of action for my family and me. Within a few days of the accident I sat down with family and friends to discuss how I was going to face my grief, manage my home, and raise my children.

On the other hand, I have a cousin, Leanna, with multiple myeloma, an incurable form of cancer. Her loss has been gradual and subtle, as it will probably continue to be. The landscape of her life is being destroyed slowly, one square inch at a time. Her suffering lingers on and on, and pain wears her down like friction wears down metal. Little inconveniences, like walking with a cane, remind her at every turn that she is sick. She has no idea what is going to happen to her in the next three years or even in the next three months. She worries about her two teenage children and about her husband, who has Parkinson's disease. That cancer looms over her, casting an ominous shadow over her entire world.

So whose loss is worse, hers or mine? It is impossible to give an answer. Both are bad, but bad in different ways.

I lost three people whom I loved deeply and who loved me as well. Though the relationships were imperfect, as all relationships are, they were nevertheless vital and growing. As I look back now, I celebrate the relationships for what they were. I cherish the memories of the four years I had with Diana Jane, the twenty years of marriage I enjoyed with Lynda, and the forty-one years I knew my mother. My grief was and is pure and sweet. I lost precious relationships that I had and still long for with all my heart.

My divorced friends face an entirely different kind of loss. They have lost relationships they never had but wanted, or had but gradually lost. Though they may feel relieved by the divorce, they still wish things had been different. They look back on lost years, on bitter conflicts and betrayal, on the death of marriage. Anger, guilt, and regret well up when they remember a disappointing past that they will never be able to forget or escape. My break was clean; theirs messy. I have been able to continue following a direction in life I set twenty years ago; they have had to change their direction. Again the question surfaces: Is it possible to determine whose loss is worse?

It was obvious almost immediately after the accident that the line drawn between the living and the dead was clear and clean. Catherine, David, and I were bruised but not seriously hurt, while John was more severely injured. Still, he recovered soon enough. The accident did not leave me with the responsibility of having to care for a disabled loved one. I did not have to attend to injuries that might have taken months or years to heal. I was not forced into making difficult ethical decisions, such as whether to continue using life-support. The living continued to live in good health; the dead died immediately. It was unspeakably horrible watching them die, but their immediate deaths gave me the freedom to concentrate my energies on building a meaningful life and a good home under new—albeit unwanted—circumstances.

Friends of mine have experienced similar traumas, but in their cases the injuries caused disability rather than death. Those disabilities have required years of care-giving, hundreds of thousands of dollars, and constant attention. In some cases, there has been no end to the crises they face, which occur almost daily. Problems keep interrupting their lives, demanding more of their time and resources and draining them of energy. While they love their disabled family members, they also feel resentment, labor under constant exhaustion, worry about money, and wonder about the future. So I ask myself again if it is possible to quantify and compare losses.

Lynda was an unusual woman. She was gracious and energetic, simple, competent, and hospitable. She found joy in serving others, and she loved her children with all her heart. She worked hard from morning to evening, laughed far more than she cried, and delighted in ordinary life. She was good and guileless at the core of her being. I miss her as she was, not as I wished her to be. I lost a friend, a lover, and a partner. Our life had found a rhythm of its own. Nearly every night, for example, we took a break around 10:00 P.M. In the summer we sat on the porch swing and drank a soda, and in the winter we sat on the living-room sofa and drank hot chocolate. We talked about the day, discussed how the children were doing, debated issues, told stories, laughed, and cuddled. Then we prayed together. We also enjoyed common interests like camping and backpacking, reading, music, gardening, and canning fruits and vegetables. We went out on dates together biweekly. We were partners in managing our home and raising the children. Our relationship was delightfully multi-dimensional. Her absence touches almost every area of my life. I am haunted by the memories. At times I feel almost desperate to find just one part of my life that was not affected by her presence and does not therefore suffer from her absence.

I was blessed in ways others were not. I am reminded of several women who endured years of abuse in their homes, whether their husbands directed it toward them or toward their children. Such abuse violated their deepest sense of right and wrong, finally driving them to file for divorce. Now they tremble with rage and imagine taking revenge. They feel the horror of betrayal and wonder endlessly why they ever married that kind of man in the first place. They face the difficult responsibility of raising abused children, who are often hard to control because of the violation and pain they have experienced. These women find it hard to trust anyone, especially men. They often feel as if they have no one to turn to.

Is it really useful to decide whose losses are worse?

I could give many other examples. Every week I hear stories about people's pain. I have probably always heard these stories, but until I experienced loss myself, I did not listen intently to them or let those stories penetrate the protective shell around my heart. I am more sensitive to the pain now, not as oblivious and selfish as I used to be. Just this month I talked with a woman who is trying to rebuild her life after a divorce, for which she filed after learning that her husband had sexually abused her daughters. I talked with another woman whose husband was recently killed in a plane crash. I heard about three women who are battling breast cancer. I met with a couple whose daughter was the survivor of an automobile accident that took the life of a passenger. I heard about a man who has struggled with unemployment or professional frustration for many years now. I learned of a couple who have exhausted every medical option in their battle against infertility. I know of a man whose business is on the brink of bankruptcy. I heard about an elderly couple who recently inherited their five grandchildren, all under the age of five, because their daughter-in-law decided that she did not want them anymore and their son is incapable of caring for them. Everywhere there is pain, human misery, and tragedy.

Catastrophic loss of whatever kind is always bad, only bad in different ways. It is impossible to quantify and to compare. The very attempt we often make in quantifying losses only exacerbates the loss by driving us to two unhealthy extremes. On the one hand, those coming out on the losing end of the comparison are deprived of the validation they need to identify and experience the loss for the bad thing it is. They sometimes feel like the little boy who just scratched his finger but cried too hard to receive much sympathy. Their loss is dismissed as unworthy of attention and recognition. On the other hand, those coming out on the winning end convince themselves that no one has suffered as much as they have, that no one will ever understand them, and that no one can offer lasting help. They are the ultimate victims. So they indulge themselves with their pain and gain a strange kind of pleasure in their misery.

Whose loss is worse? The question begs the point. Each experience of loss is unique, each painful in its own way, each as bad as everyone else's but also different. No one will ever know the pain I have experienced because it is my own, just as I will never know the pain you may have experienced. What good is quantifying loss? What good is comparing? The right question to ask is not, "Whose is worse?" It is to ask, "What meaning can be gained from suffering, and how can we grow through suffering?" That is the question I want to explore in the rest of this book.

Darkness Closes In

Die before you die. There is no chance after.

C. S. Lewis

Sudden and tragic loss leads to terrible darkness. It is as inescapable as nightmares during a high fever. The darkness comes, no matter how hard we try to hold it off. However threatening, we must face it, and we must face it alone.

Darkness descended on me shortly after the accident. I spent the first seventy-two hours caring for John, my two-year-old son, who was screaming from the pain of a broken femur and fighting the confinement of traction. I was inundated with telephone calls and visitors. Every voice and face called forth more tears and demanded the retelling of the story. I had to plan memorial services. I also had to care for my two older children, who were terrified and confused by the accident, having been pushed, as it were, out of their cozy home into a blizzard of pain. During those first busy days, however, I was rational enough to know that darkness loomed ahead and that I would soon descend into it.

That occasion came on the day of the interment. I chose to bury my mother Grace, my wife Lynda, and my daughter Diana Jane together in a cemetery in Lynden, Washington, where my mother grew up and retired and where my sister lives. It has always been a home away from home to me, as it was for Lynda. The day before their burial I decided, for a reason still unknown to me, to view their bodies once—and alone. I stayed up the entire night before that visit, sleepless because of the dread I felt. The accident kept replaying itself in my mind like a horror movie repeating its most gruesome scene. I felt I was on the edge of insanity.

The next morning I visited the funeral home and stared in disbelief at three open coffins before me. At that moment I felt myself slipping into a black hole of dread and oblivion. I was afloat in space, utterly alone among billions of nameless, distant stars. People seemed to recede from sight until they appeared to be standing far away, on some distant horizon. I had trouble hearing what people were saying, their voices were so faint. Never have I experienced such anguish and emptiness. It was my first encounter with existential darkness, though it would not be my last.

I had a kind of waking dream shortly after that, caused, I am sure, by that initial experience of darkness. I dreamed of a setting sun. I was frantically running west, trying desperately to catch it and remain in its fiery warmth and light. But I was losing the race. The sun was beating me to the horizon and was soon gone. I suddenly found myself in the twilight. Exhausted, I stopped running and glanced with foreboding over my shoulder to the east. I saw a vast darkness closing in on me. I was terrified by that darkness. I wanted to keep running after the sun, though I knew that it was futile, for it had already proven itself faster than I was. So I lost all hope, collapsed to the ground, and fell into despair. I thought at that moment that I would live in darkness forever. I felt absolute terror in my soul.

A few days later I talked about the dream with a cousin of mine, who is a minister and a poet. He mentioned a poem by John Donne that turns on the point that, though east and west seem farthest removed on a map, they eventually meet on a globe. What therefore appears as opposites—east and west—in time come together, if we follow one or the other long enough and far enough. Later my sister, Diane, told me that the quickest way for anyone to reach the sun and the light of day is not to run west, chasing after the setting sun, but to head east, plunging into the darkness until one comes to the sunrise.

I discovered in that moment that I had the power to choose the direction my life would head, even if the only choice open to me, at least initially, was either to run from the loss or to face it as best I could. Since I knew that darkness was inevitable and unavoidable, I decided from that point on to walk into the darkness rather than try to outrun it, to let my experience of loss take me on a journey wherever it would lead, and to allow myself to be transformed by my suffering rather than to think I could somehow avoid it. I chose to turn toward the pain, however falteringly, and to yield to the loss, though I had no idea at the time what that would mean.

Giving myself to grief proved to be hard as well as necessary. It happened in both spontaneous and intentional ways. I could not always determine the proper time and setting for tears, which occasionally came at unexpected and inconvenient moments, such as in the middle of a college class I was teaching or during a conversation. I was surprised to see how inoffensive that was to others. If anything, my display of grief invited them to mourn their own losses, and it made the expression of sorrow a normal and natural occurrence in daily life.

Still, I tried to reserve time and space in my life for solitude so that I could descend into the darkness alone. Late in the evening, well after the children were in bed, proved to be the best time for me. Sometimes I listened to music—mostly requiems, Gregorian chants, and other choral works; and sometimes I wrote in my journal or read good books. But mostly I sat in my rocking chair and stared into space, reliving the accident and remembering the people I lost. I felt anguish in my soul and cried bitter tears.

I wanted to pray but had no idea what to say, as if struck dumb by my own pain. Groans became the only language I could use, if even that, but I believed it was language enough for God to understand. I remember reading what the apostle Paul wrote in the book of Romans—that sometimes, when overcome by suffering, we do not know how to pray. But, Paul said, our dumbness before God is not offensive to him or indicative of a lack of faith. Instead, it is an invitation for God to draw near and to intercede for us "with groans that words cannot express,"[1] like a good mother does when holding a distraught child on her lap.

This nightly solitude, as painful and demanding as it was, became sacred to me because it allowed time for genuine mourning and intense reflection. It also gave me freedom during the day to invest my energy into teaching and caring for my children. I struggled with exhaustion, as I do now. But somehow I found the strength—God's gift to me, I think—to carry on despite getting so little sleep.

My decision to enter the darkness had far-reaching consequences, both positive and negative. It was the first step I took toward growth, but it was also the first step I took toward pain. I had no idea then how tumultuous my grief would be. I did not know the depths of suffering to which I would descend. For months I kept staring at the accident and reliving its trauma. Though I knew intuitively that I had to look at it, I still recoiled at the horror of the scene of death I had witnessed. Catherine and David talked about the accident too, and they surprised everyone by how thoroughly they remembered even little details. I also suffered from acute depression, which, on top of the frustration, bewilderment, and exhaustion, became an unwelcome and obtrusive companion of mine for many months. My world was as fragile as the lives of the loved ones whom I had lost.

That sense of darkness so preoccupied me that I found myself unable to concentrate on mundane responsibilities. I became a robot programmed to perform certain functions that I was able to do quite well because of habits developed over many years. At the end of the day I would look back and remember what I had done, as if my body, not the real me, had done it. There was a radical split between the self that did my work and the self that watched me from the shadows. My schedule was packed with responsibilities at work and at home. I taught classes at the college, advised students, attended meetings, and then returned home to cook meals, fold laundry, and spend time with my children. I performed these duties because I had to. But I looked at life like a man having an out-of-body experience.

The darkness persisted for a long time; it persists even to this day as I discover new dimensions of the loss. For example, I learned early on that I did not even have the luxury or convenience of mourning the loss of my loved ones as a group. Instead, I had to mourn them as separate individuals. As my grief over one loss would subside, grief over another would emerge. If it was not one birthday I wanted to celebrate, it was another. If one piece of music awakened sorrow for Lynda, another would awaken sorrow for Diana or my mother. I had to face what felt like one wave of sorrow after another. I could not get away from it, no matter what I tried. The pain was relentless, like midday heat in the Sahara.

But that is only half the story. The decision to face the darkness, even if it led to overwhelming pain, showed me that the experience of loss itself does not have to be the defining moment of our lives. Instead, the defining moment can be *our response* to the loss. It is not what happens *to* us that matters as much as what happens *in* us. Darkness, it is true, had invaded my soul. But then again, so did light. Both contributed to my personal transformation.

My first awareness of change within me came as I began to reflect on how I performed the mundane responsibilities from which I felt so alienated. Though I was not completely alive to them, I was able at least to think about them, if only from a distance. I was struck by how wonderful ordinary life is. Simply being alive became holy to me. As I saw myself typing exams, chatting with a student on the way to class, or tucking one of my children into bed, I sensed I was beholding something sacred. My encounters with students presented astonishing opportunities to listen and encourage. Bedtime with Catherine, David, and John allowed me to convey the blessing and love of God to them. I was not yet fully alive to these ordinary moments, but I began to glimpse how profound they were.

In other words, though I experienced death, I also experienced life in ways that I never thought possible before—not after the darkness, as we might suppose, but *in* the darkness. I did not go through pain and come out the other side; instead, I lived in it and found within that pain the grace to survive and eventually grow. I did not get over the loss of my loved ones; rather, I absorbed the loss into my life, like soil receives decaying matter, until it became a part of who I am. Sorrow took up permanent residence in my soul and enlarged it. I learned gradually that the deeper we plunge into suffering, the deeper we can enter into a new, and different, life—a life no worse than before and sometimes better. A willingness to face the loss and to enter into the darkness is the first step we must take. Like all first steps, it is probably the most difficult and takes the most time.

There is little we can do to protect ourselves from these losses. They are as inevitable as old age, wrinkled skin, aching bones, and fading memory. There is much we can do, however, to determine how to respond to them. We do not always have the freedom to choose the roles we must play in life, but we can choose how we are going to play the roles we have been given.

Choice is therefore the key. We can run from the darkness, or we can enter into the darkness and face the pain of loss. We can indulge ourselves in self-pity, or we can empathize with others and embrace their pain as our own. We can run away from sorrow and drown it in addictions, or we can learn to live with sorrow. We can nurse wounds of having been cheated in life, or we can be grateful and joyful, even though there seems to be little reason for it. We can return evil for evil, or we can overcome evil with good. It is this power to choose that adds dignity to our humanity and gives us the ability to transcend our circumstances, thus releasing us from living as mere victims. These choices are *never easy*. Though we can and must make them, we will make them more often than not only after much agony and struggle.

Many years ago I read Viktor Frankl's *Man's Search for Meaning*, a book that explores what the author discovered from personal experience about the power of choice, especially in the face of terrible loss and darkness. I reread the book two years after the accident, and I understood as never before what he had believed and argued so eloquently. During his years in Nazi death camps during World War II, Frankl observed that the prisoners who exercised the power to choose how they would respond to their circumstances displayed dignity, courage, and inner vitality. They found a way to *transcend* their suffering. Some chose to believe in God in spite of all the evidence to the contrary. They chose to expect a good tomorrow, though there was little promise of one. They chose to love, however hateful the environment in which they lived.

In other words, they refused to yield ultimate power to their captors and circumstances. Though the world was horrible to them, they identified with another world—a world inside themselves, over which they had some control. They affirmed that they were more than the product of their circumstances. As Frankl observed, these few people tried "turning life into an inner triumph" and so grew spiritually beyond themselves.[2]

It became clear to Frankl that "the sort of person the prisoner became was the result of an inner decision, and not the result of camp influences alone." In the end he asserts: "The experiences of camp life show that man does have a choice of action. There were enough examples, often of a heroic nature, which proved that apathy could be overcome, irritability suppressed. Man can preserve a vestige of spiritual freedom, of independence of mind, even in such terrible conditions of psychic and physical stress."[3] Frankl concluded that these prisoners transcended their circumstances because they found meaning in their suffering. "If there is meaning in life at all, then there must be a meaning in suffering. Suffering is an ineradicable part of life, even as fate and death. Without suffering and death human life cannot be complete."[4]

It was this power to choose that kept the prisoners alive, Frankl noted. They directed their energies inwardly and paid attention to what was happening in their souls. They learned that tragedy can increase the soul's capacity for darkness and light, for pleasure as well as for pain, for hope as well as for dejection. The soul contains a capacity to know and love God, to become virtuous, to learn truth, and to live by moral conviction. The soul is elastic, like a balloon. It can grow larger through suffering. Loss can enlarge its capacity for anger, depression, despair, and anguish, all natural and legitimate emotions whenever we experience loss. Once enlarged, the soul is also capable of experiencing greater joy, strength, peace, and love. What we consider opposites—east and west, night and light, sorrow and joy, weakness and strength, anger and love, despair and hope, death and life—are no more mutually exclusive than winter and sunlight. The soul has the capacity to experience these opposites, even at the same time.

Nicholas Wolterstorff, a philosopher who teaches at Yale, lost his adult son in a tragic mountain-climbing accident a number of years ago. He kept a journal of his experience of grief, which he later published under the title *Lament for a Son.* He came to a conclusion similar to Frankl's. At one point in the book he comments on his own experience of pain:

> And sometimes, when the cry is intense, there emerges a radiance which elsewhere seldom appears: a glow of courage, of love, of insight, of selflessness, of faith. In that radiance we see best what humanity was meant to be. . . . In the valley of suffering, despair and bitterness are brewed. But there also character is made. The valley of suffering is the vale of soul-making.[5]

It is therefore not true that we become less through loss—unless we allow the loss to make us less, grinding our soul down until there is nothing left but an external self entirely under the control of circumstances. Loss can also make us more. In the darkness we can still find the light. In death we can also find life. It depends on the choices we make. Though these choices are difficult and rarely made in haste or with ease, we can nevertheless make them. Only when we choose to pay attention to our souls will we learn how much more there is to life than the external world around us, however wonderful or horrible that world is. We will discover the world within. Yet such attention to the soul does not have to engender self-absorption. If anything, it eventually turns us toward the world again and makes us more compassionate and just than we might otherwise have been.

Not that the choices we make will always have happy results. That is especially true when we choose to face our losses squarely. When we plunge into darkness, it is *darkness* we experience. We feel pain, anguish, sorrow, and despair, and we experience the ugliness, meanness, and absurdity of life. We brood as well as hope, rage as well as surrender, doubt as well as believe. We are apathetic as often as we are hopeful, and sorrowful before we are joyful. We both mourn deeply and live well. We experience the ambivalence of living simultaneously in the night and in the light.

The choice to enter the darkness, then, does not lead us along an easy course. The darkness is not dispelled as quickly as it is for frightened children who, scrambling to find the light switch in a pitch-black basement, erase their fears the moment light floods the room. The darkness lingers for a long time, perhaps for the rest of our earthly lives. Even if we really do overcome our own pain (which is doubtful in my mind), we nevertheless find ourselves more sensitive to the pain of others and more aware of the darkness that envelops the world. The choice to enter the darkness does not ensure we ever completely come out the other side. I am not sure we can or should.

But is it possible to live this way? Is it possible to feel sorrow for the rest of our lives and yet to find joy at the same time? Is it possible to enter the darkness and still to live an ordinary, productive life? Loss requires that we live in a *delicate tension.* We must mourn, but we must also go on living. We might feel that the world has stopped, though it never does. Grass keeps growing, bills continue to mount, houses get dirty, children need raising, jobs must be done, people must be cared for. It was obviously impossible for me to express sorrow every time I felt sorrowful. I did not want to surrender myself completely to the whims and indulgences of raw emotion, and I faced responsibilities that could not be put off indefinitely. I cried occasionally in public settings, and I still do. But even then I regained composure quickly and carried on with normal activities, whether at work or at home.

After all, I *had* to care for my children, for obvious reasons. But I also *had* to work for my own emotional well-being. My professional life gave me an opportunity to function in a world that had not been directly affected by the tragedy, as my home had been. Moreover, I had close friends at the college who encouraged me to mourn and who mourned with me. My loss became so much a part of the working environment of my circle of colleagues that it was not unusual for us to pause briefly for tears and reflection during a meeting before proceeding to finish the mundane matters that had to be addressed. I learned to live and mourn simultaneously.

After three years, I continue to live in that tension. But there is a significant difference now. The sorrow I feel has not disappeared, but it has been integrated into my life as a painful part of a healthy whole. Initially, my loss was so overwhelming to me that it was the dominant emotion—sometimes the only emotion—I had. I felt like I was staring at the stump of a huge tree that had just been cut down in my backyard. That stump, which sat all alone, kept reminding me of the beloved tree that I had lost. I could think of nothing but that tree. Every time I looked out the window, all I could see was that stump. Eventually, however, I decided to do something about it. I landscaped my backyard, reclaiming it once again as my own. I decided to keep the stump there, since it was both too big and too precious to remove. Instead of getting rid of it, I worked around it. I planted shrubs, trees, flowers, and grass. I laid out a brick pathway and built two benches. Then I watched everything grow. Now, three years later, the stump remains, still reminding me of the beloved tree I lost. But the stump is surrounded by a beautiful garden of blooming flowers and growing trees and lush grass. Likewise, the sorrow I feel remains, but I have tried to create a landscape around the loss so that what was once ugly is now an integral part of a larger, lovely whole.

My own catastrophic loss thus taught me the incredible power of choice—to enter the darkness and to feel sorrow, as I did after the accident, even as I continued to work and to care for people, especially my children. I wanted to gain as much as I could from the loss without neglecting ordinary responsibilities. I wanted to integrate my pain into my life in order to ease some of its sting. I wanted to learn wisdom and to grow in character. I had had enough of destruction, and I did not want to respond to the tragedy in a way that would exacerbate the evil I had already experienced. I knew that running from the darkness would only lead to greater darkness later on. I also knew that my soul had the capacity to grow—to absorb evil and good, to die and live again, to suffer abandonment and find God. In choosing to face the night, I took my first steps toward the sunrise.

The Silent Scream of Pain

One learns of the pain of others by suffering one's own pain, my father would say, by turning inside oneself, by finding one's own soul. And it is important to know of pain, he said.

CHAIM POTOK

People who suffer loss feel unspeakable pain. At times it seems almost unbearable.

I have often told myself, not always convincingly, that pain is a gift, a sure sign that we are alive. Only the dead feel no pain, and that includes dead people who, though still alive, have rejected love and goodness and sorrow for so long that they have lost the ability to feel anything.

Pain is a gift because it shows we have a capacity to feel, whether pain in the body or pain in the soul. Physical pain demonstrates the capacity we have in our senses to experience the negative side of life in the world. Our nerves give us messages about the world, warning us of its dangers as well as informing us of its delights. Pain therefore is the flip side of pleasure. The nerves that tell us of one also tell us of the other. The eye that blinks under the glare of a bright light also gazes in wonder at a mountain peak or meadow of wildflowers. The nose that signals the scent of a dead animal under the crawl space of our house also draws us into the kitchen where bread is baking. The mouth that makes us spit out spoiled food also relishes the taste of our favorite flavor of ice cream. Ears that cringe at the wail of a siren also listen with pleasure to a Beethoven symphony.

The index finger is a marvel of well-tuned nerves, an instrument of remarkable precision. It can, for example, produce a wide variety of sounds on a violin under the guidance of a virtuoso. It can give us an infinite range of sensations, from the softness of a feather to the prickle of a cactus. It can communicate love when it strokes the hair of a lover or rubs the back of a friend.

But the index finger can also scream at us. Its capacity for pleasure is equal only to its capacity for pain. The same nerves communicate both sensations. A sliver in the foot may hurt, but nothing like a sliver in the finger. A burn hurts anywhere on the body, but in few places will it hurt as much as it does on the index finger. It commands us to do something to mitigate or eliminate the pain.

Hansen's disease (also known as leprosy) is deadly because it keeps the nerves from informing a person of pain. Thus, a sliver under the nail of a person afflicted with this disease does not make the nerves scream. The person does not know enough, consequently, to remove the sliver and cannot favor the sore finger as it heals. Little injuries can therefore become big ones over time. Sores become infected, infections turn ugly, and soon the finger is gone—all because the nerves fail to communicate pain.

What is true in the body is also true in the soul. The pain of loss is severe because the pleasure of life is so great; it demonstrates the supreme value of what is lost. The screaming pain I feel at the loss of my mother, my wife, and my daughter reflects the pure pleasure I felt in knowing them. I cannot have one without the other, for both show what the soul is capable of feeling, sometimes simultaneously.

In my experience the initial pain of loss was periodic, and I had the energy and will to fight it. I fought the pain, for example, by *denying* it. For a while it all seemed dream-like to me, hardly real, like something I read in a sad story and then immediately forgot. I tried to manage our home in the same way it was managed before, as if nothing had ever happened. I kept busy and productive so that I would not have the time and space to let the pain in. I dismissed my grief as a brief interlude in an otherwise normal, healthy, happy life.

Friends who have faced tragedy tell similar stories. A couple whose first child was born with severe disabilities believed for months that a sudden "miracle" would solve their daughter's health problems. One woman I know ignored her loss of a husband, put a smile on her face, and tried to convince herself that it was really not so bad after all. Whenever friends asked her how she was getting along, she replied, "Just great. Couldn't be better." Whenever they asked if they could help out, she said, "No, no. I'm doing just fine." A recently divorced friend of mine started new projects, set new goals, and took on new responsibilities until his time and energy were completely absorbed by busyness. He, too, refused at first to face the loss.

Denial puts off what should be faced. People in denial refuse to see loss for what it is, something terrible that cannot be reversed. They dodge pain rather than confront it. But their unwillingness to face pain comes at a price. Ultimately it diminishes the capacity of their souls to grow bigger in response to pain. They make the same mistake as patients who, following major surgery, refuse to get out of bed and put damaged muscles back to work. They pretend nothing is wrong and tell everyone that they are feeling wonderful. But denial of their problem causes muscles to atrophy until they cannot get out of bed at all. In the end denial leads to a greater loss.

When she was only four, my mother lost her mother to kidney failure during the influenza epidemic of 1919–20. The style of grieving back then, so my mother told me, was to pretend that the loss never occurred or that the person who died never existed in the first place. This form of denial still exists today. Pictures are never hung, names never spoken, sadness never expressed, tears never shed, stories never told. Pain is dealt with by not dealing with it at all.

I also fought the pain by *bargaining*, as if I could escape it through skillful negotiation. I thought about replacement relationships that could help me make the transition quickly and conveniently, but then I faced disappointment when two relationships fizzled during the first year as quickly as they had begun. I considered finding a new life for myself by moving and starting a different job so that I could escape the hellish life I was forced to live after the accident. I also imagined having the power to live that tragic day over again, changing the sequence of events that led to the accident. "If only," I thought to myself, "we had lingered longer at the powwow, or stopped to change the seating in the minivan, or waited two more seconds at a stop sign."

Moreover, I tried to drown the pain by *indulging* my appetites. I spent a great deal of time sitting alone the first months after the accident. The silence and solitude comforted me. But there was one period, about two months long, in which I broke that routine of seeking solitude by watching television almost every night from 10:00 P.M. to 2:00 A.M. I simply could not face my unbearable loneliness. I did not want to crawl into an empty bed or think about why it was empty in the first place. I was tempted to indulge other appetites as well, but close friends and family would not let me get away with it. They cared so much for me that they kept encouraging me to stay true to my convictions.

Many people form addictions after they experience loss. Loss disrupts and destroys the orderliness and familiarity of their world. They feel such desperation and disorientation in the face of this obliteration of order that they go berserk on binges. They saturate their senses with anything that will satisfy them in the moment because they cannot bear to think about the long-term consequences of loss. So they watch television every moment they can, work sixty hours a week, drink too much alcohol, go on a sexual rampage, eat constantly, or spend their money carelessly. In so doing, they hold suffering at a distance.

I resisted the pain, finally, by *venting anger*. I thought that revenge would somehow help me mitigate my suffering. I wanted someone to pay the price for the loss. I wished the alleged driver of the other car would be imprisoned for life or savagely murdered, as if more pain in him would mean less pain in us. I remember conversations with my children in which they expressed similar rage at the "murderer" of their mother, sister, and grandmother. "I hope he suffers in hell," one of them yelled. "I hope someone hurts him as much as he hurt us." "I hope God punishes him." Sometimes I even wanted the whole world to suffer. I felt no grief at all when I read or heard stories of the sufferings of other people. "We have suffered," I muttered cynically under my breath. "Why shouldn't they suffer?"

I was angry at God, too. At times I scoffed at the vain notion of praying to God or, conversely, of cursing God, as if one or the other would make any difference. At other times I cried out to God in utter anguish of soul. "How could you do this to innocent people? To my children? To me?" Sometimes I turned that anger toward my children, lashing out at them when they disobeyed. Or I turned it toward myself, feeling the guilt of having survived the accident while others, whom I considered more worthy of life than me, had died.

A few friends cautioned me about this anger, but I assumed that God was big enough to tolerate my anger and compassionate enough to understand. If God was patient with Job, I reasoned, he would be patient with me too. Besides, my anger was problem enough in itself, for I knew that anger can turn easily into bitterness. I did not want to exacerbate that problem by believing that God was so fragile that he could not absorb my anger but would turn against me instead. I found comfort in many of the Psalms that express anguish and anger before God. I see now that my faith was becoming an ally rather than an enemy because I could vent anger freely, even toward God, without fearing retribution.

Anger, like denial or bargaining or binges, is simply another way of deflecting the pain, holding it off, fighting back at it. We refuse to let the pain in and experience it for the hell it is. But the pain of loss is unrelenting. It stalks and chases until it catches us. It is as persistent as wind on the prairies, as constant as cold in the Antarctic, as erosive as a spring flood. It will not be denied and there is no escape from it. In the end denial, bargaining, binges, and anger are mere attempts to deflect what will eventually conquer us all. Pain will have its day because loss is undeniably, devastatingly real.

These initial responses to loss are natural, powerful, and even legitimate. They send a signal that something is desperately wrong in our lives. They are like a fever, which always points beyond itself to a deeper problem—sickness in the body. These responses prompt us to look at that deeper problem and see what makes life seem so ominous and terrible to us. But they can also keep us from facing it. That is why these responses, however natural, can deceive us, appearing to provide a way of escape from the problem rather than points of entry into the problem. We must therefore pay attention to them but not fool ourselves into thinking that they are merely stages on our way out of the predicament.

I did not find it helpful, therefore, nor did I find it true in my experience, to identify these various responses as "stages" through which I had to pass on my way to "recovery." For one thing, I have still not moved beyond these stages, and I am not sure I ever will. I still feel anger, I still want to bargain with God, I still face the temptation of indulging my appetites, and I still want to deny that the tragedy is true. Not that I feel the urge to escape as intensely as I used to, but that is because my internal capacity to live with loss has grown. I have more perspective now; I have more confidence in my ability to endure.

The problem with viewing these avenues of escape as stages is that it raises the false expectation that we go through them only once. Again, that has not been true for me. I have revisited them again and again. If anything, I have not moved beyond these stages but *below* them. I have learned that they were desperate attempts to avoid having to face the real problem, which I fought off as long as I could. I finally became so exhausted trying to run from the real problem that I simply gave up. In the end I was forced to address the problem of life's mortality—*my* mortality—which for a time made me profoundly depressed.

I remember the first time I realized I had no fight left. It began on the one-year anniversary of the accident. I felt a nervous agitation come on, a brooding anxiety. I sensed that something was wrong, but apprehension of it eluded me—as if I had misplaced something important and had forgotten not only where I had misplaced it but what I had misplaced in the first place. Over the next month I became increasingly restless. Eventually I started to feel a tremor inside myself, not only in my body but also deep down in my soul. I sensed that I was close to a breakdown.

I learned later that I had become profoundly depressed. Only then did I discover a language to describe my own clinical state. That language came from William Styron's book *Darkness Visible*, which tells the story of his own descent into depression.[1] Unlike physical pain, which usually points to some concrete abnormality like a broken leg, the pain of depression reflects an abnormality that cannot be so easily observed or explained. Like a headache, it appears as a phantom pain that one might decide to ignore or overcome. But willing an end to depression is as difficult as healing a broken heart. Human strength alone is insufficient for the task.

Like Styron, I found depression completely debilitating. It took Herculean strength for me to get out of bed in the morning. I was fatigued all day long, yet at night I was sleepless. I would lie awake by the hour, feeling the torment of a darkness that no one could see but me. I had trouble concentrating. I was apathetic and desireless. I could not taste food, see beauty, or touch anything with pleasure. I exacerbated the problem by telling virtually no one about my struggle. Friends and colleagues marveled at how well I was doing. But inside I was a living dead man. I finally became desperate enough to see a counselor, and for two months I took an anti-depressant so that I could function normally without losing my mind.

Clinical psychology has a vocabulary to describe depression, and it provides techniques and drugs to combat it. Still, I have found a spiritual image more helpful. The Spanish mystic, John of the Cross, wrote about something he calls "the dark night of the soul." He defines it as a depressed spiritual state into which one slips and, turning to traditional remedies—emotional fervor, spiritual discipline, rational analysis, worship, service—finds in them absolutely no help and comfort. All props are stripped away. One is left utterly alone and helpless. It is the darkness visible that Styron describes. One enters the abyss of emptiness—with the perverse twist that one is not empty of the tortured *feeling* of emptiness. If anything, this kind of emptiness fills one with dread and despair.

My friend Steve is typical of what often happens. He became a quadriplegic in a farm accident. He was twenty at the time, striving to become a major-league baseball player and engaged to be married. He spent nine months in the hospital.

During that time he refused to believe that his disability was permanent. Instead, he was confident of recovery, at least for awhile. He even joked with his physical therapist, "You wheeled me into this room, but I'm going to walk out."

But Steve has never walked out of any room. Only gradually did he begin to realize that he was going to be a quadriplegic for the rest of his life. That realization came to him in odd, torturous ways. He would feel an itch in his toe and not be able to scratch it. He would want to feed himself but not be able to pick up a spoon. He would try to roll over when uncomfortable and sore but was unable to move even one muscle in his body.

Still, it was not until he moved home from the hospital that he faced and felt the permanence of his disability. It was going home that pushed him over the edge. Glimpses of his former life reminded him of what he had lost. He saw the old basketball hoop that would never receive another one of his shots, his old baseball glove that would never snag another grounder, his old car and motorcycle that would never take him on another ride. At that moment he fell into depression, marking the beginning of his dark night.

This experience rarely follows immediately after the loss. It occurs at the end of the fight, after the denial yields to reality, the bargaining fails, the binges lead to emptiness, and the anger subsides. Then there is no will or desire left to resist the inevitable and undeniable. One is left only with deep sadness and profound depression. The divorce is final, and there is nothing to be done to win the partner back. The abuse or rape really happened, and the memory will remain for a lifetime. The cancer is terminal, and no medical miracle is going to change that. The disability is permanent, and no amount of physical therapy is going to alter the condition. The job is lost and will never be won again.

At the core of loss is the frightening truth of our *mortality.* We are creatures, made of dust. Life on earth can be and often is wonderful. But in the end all of us will die. During the last few months of Lynda's life she reached a new level of contentment and gratitude that she had not known before. She managed the home well, cared for our four children, and home schooled the oldest two. These responsibilities demanded a great deal from her, but they also brought her great joy. She was learning how to handle the frustrations and disappointments of being a wife and mother with high ideals and expectations. She was so excited about motherhood, in fact, that she suggested we adopt a child with special needs and moved us through the adoption process. The adoption agency approved us for adoption the day before the accident. She also found great satisfaction in her work as the music director of a professional children's choir, and she had been hired only a few weeks before her death as the paid soprano soloist at our church.

The night before the accident Lynda returned home from choir rehearsal at 10:00 P.M. We had hot chocolate together and crawled into bed, where we talked and laughed until 12:30 A.M. At the end of our conversation she said to me, "Jerry, I can't imagine life being any better than it is right now. It is so wonderful to me. I am overcome by the goodness of God." Less than one day later she was dead.

The accident set off a silent scream of pain inside my soul. That scream was so loud that I could hardly hear another sound, not for a long time, and I could not imagine that I would hear any sound but that scream of pain for the rest of my life.

Sailing on a Sea of Nothingness

Maybe the most sacred function of memory is just that: to render the distinction between past, present, and future ultimately meaningless; to enable us at some level of our being to inhabit that same eternity which it is said that God himself inhabits.

FREDERICK BUECHNER

I remember dreaming once of a vast ocean. I was on a ship with my three children, and we were sailing out of a safe harbor into the open sea. I turned to gaze at the harbor, which was lush with green and alive with activity. It was somehow familiar to me, and I wanted desperately to return, though for some reason I was unable, as if the ship itself had a will of its own and would not let me. Then I walked to the bow with my children and looked out over the open ocean which, from horizon to horizon, had no land or vessel to let us know there was something out there to sail toward or someone to sail with. In that moment I felt utterly alone.

Loss creates a barren present, as if one were sailing on a vast sea of nothingness. Those who suffer loss live suspended between a past for which they long and a future for which they hope. They want to return to the harbor of the familiar past and recover what was lost—good health, happy relationships, a secure job. Or they want to sail on and discover a meaningful future that promises to bring them life again—successful surgery, a second marriage, a better job. Instead, they find themselves living in a barren present that is empty of meaning. Memories of the past only remind them of what they have lost; hope for the future only taunts them with an unknown too remote even to imagine.

Memories of the past do bring joy, as I have discovered, but it takes time for memories to comfort rather than torment. A friend who lost his wife to cancer told me that at first all he could remember after her death was a sick human being who shriveled up before his eyes. Eventually he did remember the many years of marriage they had together. But even then the memories only reminded him of the depth of his loss. He wanted her and their life together back again. Though he was repulsed by the idea of forgetting those memories, he was deeply grieved whenever he remembered what he had lost. He never wanted to forget the past, yet wished at the same time he could.

I experienced a similar ambivalence. At first I could not purge the picture of the accident from my mind. For months I looked at life through shattered glass and saw the broken bodies of family members, as if the accident was a scrim through which I viewed life. Eventually, however, memories of the distant past did return, and I could begin to recollect vividly what life was like before the accident.

Lynda and I started to date while we were in college. I belonged to a party crowd during those years, while she was a prominent Christian leader on campus. Though I had become a Christian the summer before I started my junior year, it still surprised people when we became friends and later fell in love.

We were married twelve years before Catherine was born. That lapse of time gave us the freedom and leisure to build a deep friendship and to enjoy life together. Twice we worked at the same institution—at a church in the Los Angeles area, while Lynda also earned a master's degree in music, and at a liberal arts college in Iowa. We attended concerts and vacationed everywhere together. We ran and gardened together.

We also went on yearly backpacking expeditions. On one trip I contracted Rocky Mountain spotted fever, which almost killed me. On another we were chased for several hours by range cattle that our dog Plantagenet had riled up. We continued to nurture this closeness after we started a family, too. The summer before Lynda died we camped for a week at Banff National Park. We explored as much of the park as we could during the day; then at night we sat around the campfire, singing and cuddling and eating s'mores.

Lynda had endearing idiosyncrasies and broad interests. I have such a clear image in my mind of the way she expressed exasperation or disgust with an indignant, "O, for Pete's sake." I still see her working in our home with exuberance and determination, raking the lawn, sewing, painting, and wallpapering. I still hear her singing, laughing, and teasing. She had a certain way of standing, too, with her hands on the back of her hips, as if her hands were keeping her from falling over backwards. She was both idealistic and imperious, which drove me crazy sometimes. She had a rare translucence about her, due to her deep faith, and she genuinely cared about people, as evidenced by the many hundreds of people who sent cards and letters to pay her tribute after she died.

Of course I had an even longer history with my mother, Grace, whose influence in my life was, for as long as I can remember, warm and steady. When she died, I felt that I had lost my most important link to the past, as if whole chapters of my life story had been suddenly torn out.

My mother was a quiet woman. She was an attentive mother who encouraged my sister and me to succeed, disciplined us fairly, and greeted our friends graciously whenever they came over. During my last two years of high school she welcomed a dozen of my friends into our home every noon. We ate our sack lunches together and then shot pool or played basketball. She was hospitable without being intrusive. She enjoyed my friends so much, and they her, that they came for lunch even when I was gone.

My dad and she were divorced after my sister and I left home. She decided at that point to move back to her hometown, Lynden, Washington, where she worked as director of nursing at a convalescent home. She was firm and gracious at work, and she quickly earned the respect of the staff and community. After her retirement she did volunteer work, visited shut-ins, and made pots of soup and baked batches of cookies for friends and relatives. Whenever she came to visit us, she always brought along something she had canned or sewed or bought at a sale. Though she had asthma, she remained so active in her later years that Catherine and David used to call her "the outdoor grandma." To the day she died she tried to exercise every day by walking or swimming with a group of retired friends.

She also helped my sister, who was busy raising five children. She seemed to have a knack for relating best to the grandchildren who had the hardest time growing up. Still, she was devoted to them all. She relished going on hikes with them, sewing them pajamas, and talking with them. She loved to impart advice, which she communicated through pithy phrases over the phone or in letters. At the funeral the grandchildren put an insert into the bulletin containing samples of their favorite quotes taken from letters they had received from her. "Make the most of the best and the least of the worst." "The determination to keep going will be there when you need it." "It is good God gives us just one minute, hour, day at a time; otherwise it would be overwhelming." She concluded every letter she wrote to her grandchildren—and to her children, for that matter—with the same phrase: "Be kind, sweet, and considerate."

I knew Diana Jane for such a short time, only four years. So I did not have the history with her that I had with my mother and Lynda. Yet she was my daughter whom I rocked to sleep at night, read to in the morning, and wrestled with after dinner. Like any daughter with a father, she had won my heart. Of all my children, she had the most obvious idiosyncrasies, which endeared her to everyone. And she was the only one in our family who had to wear glasses, which she was forever pushing up on her nose.

She used to climb onto my lap in the early morning. After taking a few minutes to wake up, she would say affectionately and authoritatively, "Daddy! Story!" She loved to change clothes, which she did many times every day without putting any of her clothes back in the drawer, much to Lynda's frustration. She giggled often, cried loud and hard, and seemed to walk everywhere on her tiptoes. Mischievous eyes told the story of her personality. Independent and stubborn, she could get away with almost anything because she was so hard to resist and almost too cute to discipline.

These memories were, and are, beautiful to me. I cling to them as a man clings to a plank of wood while lost in the middle of the sea. But they are also troubling because they are only that—*memories.* They are vestiges of a past I will never again possess. They involve people I will never again see. I cannot live with the memories, and I cannot live without them.

Hope for the future functions similarly. It is impossible not to imagine the future, and it is equally impossible to imagine the future without using the present as material for our imagination. After doing woodworking as a hobby, for instance, you can imagine a career in carpentry. After viewing slides of New Zealand, you can imagine what it would be like to travel there. After winning your first college debate, you can dream about becoming a great trial lawyer. The problem with those who have suffered loss is that they are deprived of familiar material from the present in order to envision the future.

Much of what I had imagined for my future became impossible after the accident. Lynda and I were planning to adopt a special needs child, and we were also exploring the possibility of moving to Africa for a year to do volunteer work for a mission organization, such as Wycliffe Bible Translators. Lynda wanted to continue home schooling because she liked the idea of keeping the children home for two or three more years before they went to school. She had recently started work as the paid soprano soloist at our church, and she was busy practicing soprano solos for Handel's *Messiah*. In fact, my mother had come to visit us for the weekend to help Lynda shop for a new formal dress for the performance. We were becoming more established in Spokane, too. I had just started coaching soccer, and both of us were active in Habitat for Humanity, an organization committed to provide simple and affordable housing for the working poor.

Then, suddenly, there was no Lynda, no Diana Jane, no Grace. How could I conceive of a future without them? The very thought was abhorrent to me. Whenever I thought about the future, I still found them there. But they were never going to be there, which only made me more aware of how devastating my loss was. Thus, like my view of past memories, my view of the future reflected an ambivalence. I remembered a past that included people I did not want to give up, and I imagined a future that excluded people I desperately wanted to keep. For a time I was deprived, therefore, of the comfort that good memories provide and of the hope that a good imagination creates.

That is why the present was so barren to me and is so hopeless for many who face tragic loss. This barrenness can be overwhelming. "Will this emptiness continue forever?" we ask ourselves. "Will I feel this way for the rest of my life?" "Am I doomed to sail forever on a vast sea of nothingness?" These questions expose the depths of sorrow to which people who suffer such loss often descend.

If the present moment threatens to remain permanently barren, then sorrow can easily turn into despair. This despair posed a particular threat to friends of mine, Andy and Mary, after their daughter Sarah was born. Mary's pregnancy was normal. She watched her diet, walked four miles a day, and enrolled in birth classes. She was as prepared for childbirth as any pregnant woman could be.

But during labor the baby showed signs of distress. By the time Sarah was born, she "looked dead," as Andy describes her now. She was immediately rushed to the ICU. Over the next several months it became clear to medical experts that she had suffered severe trauma during delivery and would be mentally disabled for life.

Now close to four years old, Sarah has never walked, talked, or fed herself. She also has cerebral palsy, and she cries much of the time. Her parents have had to endure countless nights of screaming and countless days of disruption. They have had to watch other children Sarah's age progress normally toward adulthood, thus leaving their daughter farther and farther behind. Her presence in their lives dominates and drains them. They live under marital stress, worry about their limited financial resources, and wonder how they will be able to manage caring for her in the years ahead. As each new day begins, they wake up to find loss "staring them in the face." They want desperately to care for Sarah, but they are not quite sure how best to do it. They feel sorrow for Sarah and for themselves. What will happen to her? What will happen to them?

Andy and Mary will never "recover" from their loss. Nor can they. Can anyone really expect to recover from such tragedy, considering the value of what was lost and the consequences of that loss? Recovery is a misleading and empty expectation. We recover from broken limbs, not amputations. Catastrophic loss by definition precludes recovery. It will transform us or destroy us, but it will never leave us the same. There is no going back to the past, which is gone forever, only going ahead to the future, which has yet to be discovered. Whatever that future is, it will, and must, include the pain of the past with it. Sorrow never entirely leaves the soul of those who have suffered a severe loss. If anything, it may keep going deeper.

But this depth of sorrow is the sign of a healthy soul, not a sick soul. It does not have to be morbid and fatalistic. It is not something to escape but something to embrace. Jesus said, "Blessed are those who mourn, for they will be comforted."[1] Sorrow indicates that people who have suffered loss are living authentically in a world of misery, and it expresses the emotional anguish of people who feel pain for themselves or for others. Sorrow is noble and gracious. It enlarges the soul until the soul is capable of mourning and rejoicing simultaneously, of feeling the world's pain and hoping for the world's healing at the same time. However painful, sorrow is good for the soul.

Deep sorrow often has the effect of stripping life of pretense, vanity, and waste. It forces us to ask basic questions about what is most important in life. Suffering can lead to a simpler life, less cluttered with nonessentials. It is wonderfully clarifying. That is why many people who suffer sudden and severe loss often become different people. They spend more time with their children or spouses, express more affection and appreciation to their friends, show more concern for other wounded people, give more time to a worthy cause, or enjoy more of the ordinariness of life. In the film *The Doctor*, an arrogant physician who shows little regard for the real needs of his patients is transformed when he suddenly becomes a patient himself. His encounter with cancer makes him sensitive to the people whom he had previously treated only as sick bodies.

I look back with both longing and horror on that first year after the accident. Though I was overcome by grief, I was also single-minded and intensely focused. I gave myself to the concerns that were most important to me, one of which was my role as a single father. I tried to be attentive to my children. Every week I took them to music lessons. I coached my son David in soccer and took my daughter to concerts and musical theater performances. We played board games together at night, read good books aloud, skied cross-country style in the winter, and took walks and bike rides in the summer. We camped and backpacked. One summer we even had to leave Glacier National Park when a snowstorm dumped seven inches of snow on our campground!

I have had moments with the children that are ineffably meaningful to me. I was often present at the right time and had conversations with them that have become sacred events. In one instance David, then seven, crawled up on my lap late at night, long after his normal bedtime. At first he just sat there. Then, hesitatingly, he began to express rage at the drunk driver who supposedly caused the accident. He cried with anguish. He said that he wanted to punish that man and make him hurt as much as he had hurt us. He said that he wanted to make the whole world suffer so everyone would feel as bad as he did. After he stopped crying, we sat in silence for awhile. Then he said, "You know, Dad, I bet someone hurt him, too, like maybe his parents. That's why he did something to hurt us. And then I bet someone else hurt his parents. It just keeps going on and on. When will it ever stop?"

During that first year I cared little about advancement and prestige. I did my job, though not to impress other people or to get ahead. I was rarely elated by successes or depressed by failures—as if I was detached from it all. When I came up for tenure, I never wondered or worried about it. I spent time with friends because I valued being with them, and I decided what I wanted to believe because I thought it was true and right, not because it was popular or expected. I reflected on the kind of person I wanted to be, not to please others but to be true to God and myself. I enjoyed a rare kind of simplicity, freedom, and equilibrium that I may never know again. I found satisfaction in the doing of life, not in the getting done of it. Though I have not entirely lost the intensity and purity of that first year, I find my life more cluttered now with extraneous concerns and trivial worries. I do not miss the screaming pain, but I do miss the clarity and focus I had then.

Loss provides an opportunity to take inventory of our lives, to reconsider priorities, and to determine new directions. "Few people," someone once told me, "wish at seventy that they had worked more hours at the office when they were forty. If anything, they wish that they had given more time back then to family, friends, and worthy causes. They wish they had dared to say 'no' to pressure, competition, and image and 'no' to their own selfishness." As Jesus said, "What good is it for a man to gain the whole world, and yet forfeit his soul?"[2] Loss invites us to ask basic questions about ourselves. "What do I believe?" "Is there life after death?" "Is there a God?" "What kind of person am I?" "Do I really care about other people?" "How have I used my resources—my time, money, and talent?" "Where am I headed with my life?"

Deep sorrow is good for the soul for another reason too. It can make us more alive to the present moment. This notion may appear to contradict what I mentioned earlier. But perhaps the present is other than the nothingness it has sometimes seemed to be. It may be that the present contains the secret of the renewal of life we long for, as if, in looking under the surface of this vast sea of nothingness, we may find another world that is teeming with life.

Mystics have described this new way of experiencing the present. Jean-Pierre De Caussade called it "the sacrament of the present moment." Thomas Kelly identified it as "the eternal now." This view of the present makes us aware of the wonder of life itself, gives us a keen awareness of the world around us, and deepens our appreciation for each moment as it comes to us. Even in loss and grief, we can choose to embrace the miracle of each moment and receive the gifts of grace that come to us all the time. This present moment, this eternal now, is sacred because, however painful, it is the only time we have to be alive and to know God. The past is gone, the future not yet here. But the present is alive to us.

Recently I watched the film *Grand Canyon.* The movie pulses with the chaotic life of Los Angeles. It tells the story of how several people, somehow linked together, respond to life as it comes randomly at them. It shows scenes of violence and cruelty, but also of grace and beauty. The characteristic responses to this randomness depend on their vision, what they want to see, and what they want life to be in the present moment.

The heroine of the story, Claire, stumbles on an abandoned baby while jogging one day and decides to adopt her. She tells her husband, Mack, that her accidental discovery of the baby was no accident but a miracle. He complains of a headache during their conversation, and she upbraids him: "If I am right, and these are miracles, then it is an inappropriate response to get a headache in the presence of a miracle."

The movie uses the Grand Canyon as a metaphor for transcendence. The enormousness of the Grand Canyon helps us to see that life is more than the string of random experiences it sometimes seems to be. Transcendence makes our tragedies look smaller and opens us to the possibility that life is more than tragedy and that there is also grace, which is given in the miracle of the present moment.

Life in the present moment has become a gift to me. A year after the accident I went cross-country skiing in the Cascade Mountains. It was very cold, maybe ten below zero. A foot of new snow had fallen. It was 10:00 P.M., and the moon was full. I skied for two hours. The rhythm of the skis mesmerized me and gave me a feeling of order and calmness. When I stopped, as I occasionally did, I experienced the absolute silence of a winter's evening and watched the snow glisten under the bright moon. I was so alive to the moment, so carefree and content, that I quivered with delight.

During those hours on the trail I was reminded of Roald Amundsen, the Norwegian explorer who was the first person to reach the South Pole. His small party stopped him when he reached his goal and asked him, as their leader, to say a few words about his great feat. He said that he had no profound thoughts at that moment, no rapturous feelings, only that it was "so good to be alive." It occurred to me at that moment on the trail that it might be possible for me to live that way all the time, and I have tried to ever since.

Perhaps "try" is not quite the right word, since trying hard to live seems to contradict the idea that life—life in its ordinariness and dailyness—is a gift. Many times over the past two years I have started to laugh, for no apparent reason. I observe my children arguing and suddenly start to laugh. Or I straighten up the house and see piles of laundry in the utility room, and I start to laugh. Or I think about the peculiar circumstances of my life and, once again, I start to laugh. It is a laughter born out of the sheer joy of being alive to the present, and sometimes crazy, moment.

I hired a part-time nanny nine months after the accident. Monica was twenty-two at the time, hardly experienced in such a job but eager to learn and full of love and idealism. She has become a member of the household, like a daughter to me and like an older sister to my children. Three months later I invited a boarder to move in to help occasionally with child care and to provide the family with extra income. Todd, like Monica, won our hearts. Both of them were students of mine at the college and casual friends. They soon became close friends by spending so much time with each other in our home—so close, in fact, that they fell in love and got married. I performed the wedding, John was the ring bearer, Catherine and David candle-lighters. The growth of their relationship was another miracle to me. It was like a flower growing out of ashes. There have been many such flowers, all gifts of grace.

Gifts of grace come to all of us. But we must be ready to see and willing to receive these gifts. It will require a kind of sacrifice, the sacrifice of believing that, however painful our losses, life can still be good—good in a different way than before, but nevertheless good. I will never recover from my loss and I will never get over missing the ones I lost. But I still cherish life—Monica and Todd, my children and the privilege of raising them, deep friendships, service to college and community, moments of worship and quiet reflection, good books to read, summer hobbies. Moreover, I will always want the ones I lost back again. I long for them with all my soul. But I still celebrate the life I have found because they are gone. I have lost, but I have also gained. I lost the world I loved, but I gained a deeper awareness of grace. That grace has enabled me to clarify my purpose in life and rediscover the wonder of the present moment.

The Amputation of the Familiar Self

Who am I? This or the other?
Am I one person today and tomorrow another?
Am I both at once? A hypocrite before others,
and before myself a contemptible woebegone weakling?
Or is something within me still like a beaten army fleeing
in disorder from victory already achieved?
Who am I? They mock me, these lonely questions of mine.
Whoever I am, Thou knowest, O God, I am thine!

DIETRICH BONHOEFFER

Our sense of personal identity depends largely on the roles we play and the relationships we have. What we do and who we know contributes significantly to how we understand ourselves. Catastrophic loss is like undergoing an amputation of our identity. It is not like the literal amputation of a limb. Rather, it is more like the amputation of the self from the self. It is the amputation of the self as professional, if one has lost a job. Or the self as husband, if one has lost a spouse through divorce or death. Or the self as an energetic and productive person, if one has lost good health. Or the self as a respected member of the community, if one has lost reputation. Or the self as pure and innocent, if one has been raped or abused. It is the amputation of the self we once were or wanted to be, the self we can no longer be or become.

I still think of myself as a husband to Lynda, as a father to Diana Jane, and as a son to Grace. But the people who defined me that way, who played the role opposite me as wife, daughter, and mother, are no longer there. The self I once was, this familiar self, cries out for them, like nerves still telling me that I have a leg or an arm, though only a stump remains.

Loss thus leads to a confusion of identity. Since we understand ourselves in large measure by the roles we play and the relationships we have, we find ourselves in a vertigo when these are changed or lost. I sometimes feel like I am a stranger to myself. I am not quite sure what to do with me. It is as if I just woke up in a new house after having gone to bed the night before in familiar surroundings, and I keep tripping over furniture and walking into walls. It is a new world for me, but I act as if it were the old one. I am not a husband anymore, but neither do I perceive myself as single. I am not a father to Diana Jane anymore, though I think about her often. I am not one-half of a parent team anymore, however much I would like to be. I am a widower, a single parent, a motherless child. It is a peculiar and confusing identity.

My awareness of this amputation of the self comes to me like a reflex. Even after three years of widowhood, my psyche is still programmed to look for people who are no longer there. I crawl into bed at night and wait for Lynda to cuddle with me. I sink into the couch after the kids are in bed and half expect Lynda to join me for hot chocolate and conversation. I receive good news and want to call Lynda to tell her about it. What defines me as a person—my sexuality, my intellect, my feelings, my convictions, my plans—still searches for her like a homing pigeon for its roost. But the self I once was cannot find its old place to land. It is homeless now.

Anyone who has endured a severe loss faces similar confusion. "I used to be in sales until I lost my job two years ago," a woman says to a new friend. "*Until I lost my job.*" The words blare in her ears as she says them. They make her feel self-conscious. She is unemployed now, unable to find the same kind of job she did for twenty years. She is not what she used to be, though she still thinks of herself that way. The same could be said of others. "*I am divorced.*" "*We don't have any children.*" "*I have inoperable cancer.*" "*I lost my husband last year.*" "*I was raped.*" These phrases mean loss of identity. They refer to what we used to be but no longer are.

I have a friend whose loss precipitated a profound crisis of identity. She was not even aware of her loss until she reached her thirties and had two children. Suddenly, as if by some internal alarm clock that was set off inside her, she began to remember without any prompting from others that she had been sexually abused as a little girl. That memory terrified her. She could hardly contain the dread, panic, and rage that rose inside her.

For two weeks she refused to go outside her house. She cried often and would not see friends. Only a therapist's intervention and a mentor's friendship saved her from total collapse. She told me once that she wished she could go somewhere for a long weekend, deal with the problem, be done with it, and then return to her normal life. But, as she said to me, "it follows me wherever I go and whatever I'm doing." She distrusts men, fears for her children, and fights depression. "I'm not the same person I used to be," she confided in me. She wonders if she will ever be happy and energetic again. She knows she has lost her former identity, but she is unsure of how to find a new identity on the other side of her loss.

But it is not simply the loss of identity that causes a problem. It is also the difficult conditions under which a new identity must be formed. Catastrophic loss cannot be mitigated by replacements. One cannot escape it simply by finding a new spouse, a new job, a new life. A convenient passage to a new identity is usually out of the question. One moment my friend Steve was planning to pursue a professional baseball career; the next moment he was a quadriplegic. It is no small task to replace a baseball mitt with a wheelchair. One moment Andy and Mary were planning to raise a healthy first-born; the next moment they became parents of a mentally challenged baby. A widow I know talked with me recently about the difficulty of raising her fatherless son. There was the occasional male coach or teacher who took an interest in him, but nothing could replace the daily interaction of a father with his son.

I too find myself in circumstances that make my new identity as a widower and single father unusual and difficult. I have tried to help my children grieve—to make room for their anger, welcome their tears, listen to their complaints, create order out of chaos, and do this work of comfort in a way that is sensitive to timing and to the unique personality of each child. Yet this important task has not mitigated the demands of managing a normal household, which requires attention to an endless list of details.

I have made sacrifices in my profession, since I cannot put in the hours I used to. So I continue to fall farther and farther behind, especially in keeping up with current scholarship. My children have made sacrifices too, since they do not have two parents to give them time and attention. As Catherine said to me recently, "How am I going to be able to grow up without a mom to tell secrets to?" David and John have expressed that same longing for the kind of attention and nurture that only a mother can give. All of them wonder how our home would be affected if Diana Jane were still alive. They miss her very much too.

I have discovered that busyness and exhaustion can sabotage healing. The difficulty of my immediate circumstances only increases my awareness of the magnitude of the loss, as if I were being forced to live on the banks of a polluted river after having lived most of my life near a mountain stream in Colorado. My quest for a new identity seems repulsive to me. Do I really want the kind of life I now have? Do I really want another life in the future? Is this the kind of life I will have to live forever?

I have been told that amputees often feel phantom pains. The limb they lost still announces its presence through pain. For those who have endured irreversible loss, phantom pains of their former identity may linger for a long time. There are reminders of the former life everywhere, and they may appear in surprising ways. Thus a woman who lost her job due to "downsizing" welcomes a new neighbor, only to discover that the neighbor is a new employee at the firm that let her go. A man immobilized by cancer catches himself looking wistfully at a father shooting baskets with his two teenage daughters. A forty-year-old woman is reminded of the three babies she lost to miscarriage every time she sees a young mother holding a newborn.

In my case, it has been over three years since the accident. Yet I still awaken in the morning, wishing that I could greet Lynda. I still hear her singing the soprano solos in *Carmina Burana*, which she performed while six months pregnant. I still see visions of her canning cherries and peaches in the kitchen on a hot summer day. I still catch myself starting to perform rituals that made daily life special with her, like bringing her morning coffee while she was still in bed.

This crisis of identity, however, can lead to the formation of a new identity that integrates the loss into it. Loss creates a new set of circumstances in which we must live. When, at the right time, we are able to acknowledge the ineradicable nature of those circumstances, we can begin forging a new life for ourselves. Loss establishes a new context for life. I am a widower and single parent, whether I want to be or not. Someone else is divorced, or terminally ill, or disfigured. That is the undeniable reality of life.

Two days after the accident I had a long conversation with a few close friends and my sister and brother-in-law. First we cried and reminisced. Then we talked about the funeral. But eventually someone asked, "What are you going to do, Jerry? You have three children to raise by yourself!" We discussed child care, discipline of the children, and home management. However difficult, that conversation was necessary, as were many others, because I had to learn how to build a new life for myself and my family. My new circumstances were a given; my response was not. The tragedy became the catalyst for creative action. Under the guidance of friends and family, I began almost immediately to integrate the tragedy into a new pattern of life. Loss became a part of our story. It established the conditions under which a broken and bewildered man started to form a new identity.

I started some new traditions during the first year, like observing the anniversary of the accident by cooking Lynda's favorite dinner and paging through old photo albums in order to remember the loved ones who died. I also changed my strategy of discipline: I tried to hold the children responsible for the consequences of their choices, however good or bad. I assigned them more chores too. A year ago I hired someone to remodel our kitchen and to carpet the living room and basement. I also wallpapered a couple of bedrooms. These changes at home allowed us to put our own stamp on territory that we needed to make our own.

I kept the children in activities, such as music lessons, which they had taken before the accident. But I also encouraged them to try new activities. Just recently Catherine enrolled in a gymnastics class, and she also performed as a member of the chorus in our college's production of *Fiddler on the Roof.* We also took up cross-country skiing as a family, and during two successive January terms we lived in community with twenty students in a remote area of the Cascades, where I taught an upper-division course on the history of spirituality. So with the background already sketched in by circumstances beyond my control, I picked up a paintbrush and began, with great hesitation and distress, to paint a new portrait of our lives.

At first I was tempted to paint on a small canvas because I assumed that from that point on I would be living a small life. I wondered how I could keep the same expectations of having the good life I had before, considering the death of three people who had made it so good. Many people who suffer loss are tempted to do the same, lowering their expectations of what they will get out of life. Can any person look forward to a life that falls so far short of what he or she had planned, wanted, and expected?

A woman works hard to earn a graduate degree but finds no job in her chosen field after graduation. A father gives himself to a son and then has to give up that son to an untimely death. A wife looks forward to a lifetime of marriage and then wonders how she ended up in a divorce court. What is left to enjoy after having lost so much that was so dear? No wonder people who suffer loss often become bitter and reclusive. To think that life can still be good appears almost irreverent. How can it be good without the people or conditions that once promised to make it good? Having high expectations seems audacious and absurd.

But perhaps it is not as audacious and absurd as it seems. Expectations can remain high, as high as they were before the loss, *but only if we are willing to change their focus.* I can no longer expect to grow old with my spouse, for that path is forever closed to me. If that remains my expectation, then I will surely be disappointed. But perhaps I can expect something else that is equally good, only different. I have the opportunity and privilege, for example, to raise my children now as a single father, to learn to enjoy life and find contentment as a single man, and to gain wisdom through the experience of suffering. Again, my expectations can remain high if I am willing to adapt them to new circumstances. The scenery of my life is different now, as different as the desert is from the mountains. But it can still be beautiful, as beautiful as the desert at dusk.

I have already mentioned Andy and Mary, whose first child became severely disabled as a result of birth trauma. They had looked forward, as all new parents do, to the milestones of their baby's life—first smile, first steps, first sentence—and to the relationships that a normal child develops with parents. But their little girl is not normal. She will never walk or talk. Her presence in their home has precipitated a crisis of expectation. They do, of course, expect less of her since she is incapable of doing what most children her age can do. But they have begun to expect more of themselves. They have become extraordinarily loving and patient people through their experience, though they continue to struggle.

I have found it difficult to keep my expectations high because of the loss I suffered. I prefer the way my life was before the accident and have therefore hesitated to believe my life can be good now. I have tried to embrace my circumstances, but more often than not I have been stopped short by the limitations of my own flawed nature. I have discovered time and again how impatient I can get when my children disobey and how joyless I become when the day does not go as planned. I have learned how often my virtue and sense of purpose depend on favorable circumstances—good health, happy marriage, nice home, meaningful work, close friendships.

One incident in particular has happened too many times to count. It is the weekend. I have worked hard all week, and I am weary. I need a break. But Catherine and David are crabby. They begin to bug each other, though not enough to require a reprimand. Then John starts to whine and tattle. No one wants to go to bed (but me, of course), so they dawdle and stall for time. I nag them, but they refuse to listen. When I put pressure on, they resist. Finally I blow up, start to yell, and chase them off to bed. After they are in bed, I regret losing my patience, wish I were a better father, and long for Lynda's presence and help. I realize how far short I fall from the kind of person I want to be. I look back wistfully on a time when it seemed easier to be a parent.

Loss forces us to see the dominant role our environment plays in determining our happiness. Loss strips us of the props we rely on for our well-being. It knocks us off our feet and puts us on our backs. In the experience of loss, we come to the end of ourselves.

But in coming to the end of ourselves, we can also come to the beginning of a vital relationship with God. Our failures can lead us to grace and to a profound spiritual awakening. This process occurs frequently with those who suffer loss. It often begins when we face our own weaknesses and realize how much we take favorable circumstances for granted. When loss deprives us of those circumstances, our anger, depression, and ingratitude expose the true state of our souls, showing us how small we really are. We see that our identity is largely external, not internal.

Finally, we reach the point where we begin to search for a new life, one that depends less on circumstances and more on the depth of our souls. That, in turn, opens us to new ideas and perspectives, including spiritual ones. We feel the need for something beyond ourselves, and it begins to dawn on us that reality may be more than we once thought it to be. We begin to perceive hints of the divine, and our longing grows. To our shock and bewilderment, we discover that there is a Being in the universe who, despite our brokenness and sin, loves us fiercely. In coming to the end of ourselves, we have come to the beginning of our true and deepest selves. We have found the One whose love gives shape to our being.

My faith did not begin with the accident. Still, since then I have grown spiritually in new ways. The tragedy pushed me toward God, even when I did not want him. And in God I found grace, even when I was not looking for it. As a single parent, I have reached the point of such frustration and fatigue that I have given up trying to be a perfect parent for my children and have instead invited God to be their parent through me. I have found myself praying for them almost constantly, even asking

God to protect them from my weaknesses. As a professor, I have given up trying to read every book I feel obligated to read and have instead tried to enjoy every moment of reading or teaching as a hallowed event and every encounter with my students as a divine gift. My loss has revealed how small my life is and how limited my resources are. But it has also enabled me to see how privileged I am to be alive and how meaningful are the opportunities afforded me to serve as a parent and a teacher.

Not that I have achieved perfect contentment and gratitude. There will never be a real point of arrival. What matters is the movement forward. New circumstances require new adjustments, continued growth, and constant struggle. Soon I will have teenagers, and that will demand character, wisdom, and energy that I presently lack. New students will challenge me to adapt my methods of teaching and increase my knowledge of familiar subjects. One of Jesus' early and great followers, the apostle Paul, wrote once that it is not what we have achieved but what we are striving for that counts. "But one thing I do," he wrote. "Forgetting what is behind and straining toward what is ahead, I press on toward the goal to win the prize for which God has called me heavenward in Christ Jesus."[1]

We need someone greater than ourselves to help us forge a new identity. God is able to guide us on this quest, to help us become persons whose worth is based on grace and not on performance, accomplishments, and power. We can learn simply to be, whether we are divorced, unemployed, widowed, abused, sick, or even dying. We can allow ourselves to be loved as creatures made in God's image, though our bodies are broken, our thoughts confused, and our emotions troubled. And we can start to become hopeful that life can still be good, although never in the way it was before.

A Sudden Halt to Business As Usual

Even the saddest things can become, once we have made peace with them, a source of wisdom and strength for the journey that still lies ahead.

FREDERICK BUECHNER

A motion picture contains many picture frames, each slightly different from the one before and after, which run by fast enough on a screen to be indistinguishable from each other. The viewer sees the motion of the frames, not the individual frames themselves—unless, of course, the projector runs slow enough for the viewer to see one frame after the other, or unless it freezes on just one frame, in which case the action stops altogether and the motion picture becomes a snapshot.

We live life as if it were a motion picture. Loss turns life into a snapshot. The movement stops; everything freezes. We find ourselves looking at picture albums to remember the motion picture of our lives that once was but can no longer be.

We simply assume, quite rightly, that daily life is lived on a continuum of past to present to future. Tasks not done today can be done next Saturday. Conflicts not resolved yesterday can be addressed tomorrow. Trips not taken this summer can be taken next year. We live expecting that the circumstances of our lives—our health, our relationships, our employment—will remain roughly the same from day to day, changing only incrementally and predictably. We really *must* live that way. It is impossible to pack into one day all the living that we want to do over a lifetime. Careers, relationships, and experiences unfold only gradually over time.

Thus married couples talk about phases in their relationship—for example, the phase of romance, the phase of careers, the phase of children. Professionals talk about seasons in their careers, like the season of training and the season of idealism. Developmental theorists describe human growth in terms of psycho-social stages, like Erik Erikson's stages of trust, independence, and so forth. Life is a process. It does not happen all at once but over a period of time and through successive stages.

Loss puts a sudden halt to business as usual. Life as we experienced it and expected it to be suddenly ends. We find ourselves bewildered that there is no relationship anymore, no job, no health, no marriage, or no family. The process as we knew it ends, the continuum is disrupted, and the growth stops. The motion picture becomes a snapshot.

I have photographs of Lynda, Diana Jane, and my mother on the mantle in our living room. I still have not gotten used to seeing them there. I gaze at photographs of people I once knew and enjoyed, lived with, talked to, and held in my arms. Their pictures fall far short of what they were in real life and what real life was like with them. Immobile and lifeless, they are beautiful but dead, mere snapshots of people whom I knew as living people in the motion picture of our life together. They are poor replacements of the multi-dimensional relationships I had with them.

I am comforted by the trajectories of these relationships. We loved each other well, though imperfectly. We were building a meaningful life together. Lynda and I had just weathered a period of tension in our relationship and had entered a new period of romance. We were communicating well and finding time for each other, in spite of being so busy at work and home. Diana Jane, who consistently favored Lynda over me, was starting to attach herself to me and to demand my attention. My mother relished the times she could visit us. She always came with enthusiasm and an eagerness to serve. She was proud of me, as I was of her. Had these relationships continued, the motion picture probably would have had a happy ending. They were all headed in the right direction.

Even so I have regrets. The relationships were still flawed and incomplete. There was a lack of finality to them, as if we were in the middle of cooking a gourmet banquet that already showed promise by the smells and tastes of food in preparation but was cut short by a fire that destroyed the entire kitchen. We were becoming something better, but the relationships had not yet matured to what they could have been. For example, I had always been inclined in my marriage to demand too much from Lynda and to give too little to her. Lynda and I had also tended to follow certain patterns whenever we had a conflict. She would blame, and I would feel guilty. The only problem was that she was not always right and I was not always wrong. We both knew that too. We were striving to change that pattern when the accident occurred, and we were making good progress. I wish we had had the chance to carry on a while longer.

I have been startled by the number of people who have said to me, "There are some things I do not miss about the loved one I lost." Like relationships, people fall short of the ideal too. They have irritating idiosyncrasies, bad habits, and mean streaks. They flounder and fail. They are in process and therefore have not arrived yet. My sister and I loved our mother and miss her very much, but we feel relieved that certain elements of her personality have been happily put to rest. I feel the same about Lynda, as she would feel about me had I died instead of her. All people have flaws. All people are imperfect, which is one reason why all relationships are imperfect. When someone suffers the loss of a relationship, they lose something that is both precious and incomplete.

This problem of incompleteness is aggravated in the case of those whose relationship at the time of loss is at a low point. A spouse is killed just after an argument at home. A wife tries to work out differences with her husband but finally gives up, settling for divorce. Parents of a wayward teenager regret how much they neglected her as she was growing up. The saying may be trivial: "You can never say 'I love you' too much, because you never know when you won't be able to say it anymore," but it touches on a truth. Loss takes what we might do and turns it into what we can never do. Loss freezes life into a snapshot. We are stuck with what was instead of what could have been.

This sudden halt to business as usual constitutes the darker side of grief. It forces us to recognize the incompleteness of life and to admit our failures. Regret is therefore an unavoidable result of any loss, for in loss we lose the tomorrow that we needed to make right our yesterday or today. Regret is especially bitter because we are deprived of the very context—relationship, job, or whatever—that is needed to reverse the failure and set a new course before it is too late. Regret is bad because it is irreversible.

Virtually every person I know who has gone through a divorce has regrets—regrets about selfishness, dishonesty, criticism, coldness, temper, and manipulation. They see how different it could have been, which only exacerbates their feeling of failure. Five years, ten years, even twenty years are washed away unnecessarily. Parents of a child who has committed suicide talk about similar regrets. They realize that they did not discipline their child consistently, or they pushed material things on their son or daughter as a substitute for parental attention. Now it is too late to reverse the damage. Their child is gone forever.

People with terminal illness wonder whether better habits might have spared them from the disease. Why, they ask, did they not heed the medical warnings against smoking, overeating, poor diet, alcohol abuse, or drug addiction? Reckless or drunk drivers live with the regret of having caused the death of an innocent person because they did not say no to their appetite for speed or drink. Victims of abuse wish they had confronted the abuser or cried for help. Instead, they said nothing, endured the abuse, and let it become shame in their soul. I have talked with several friends with disabilities who have regrets because they did not make wise decisions when they had good health. One person told me that she wished she had pursued a career. Another wished he had spent more time at home with his family and less time at work.

Regret causes us to repeat a litany of "if onlys": "If only I had tried harder to make the marriage work . . . ," "If only I had forgiven him . . . ," "If only I had studied harder . . . ," "If only I had slowed down . . . ," "If only I had quit smoking . . . ," "If only I had asked him to stay home that night . . . ," "If only I had gone to the doctor sooner, when I first noticed the symptoms . . . ," "If only I had not spoken in such anger. . . ."

Regret keeps the wounds of loss from healing, putting us in a perpetual state of guilt. We think there is no forgiveness or redemption because we are deprived of the opportunity to right our wrongs. No one, for example, can bring my wife, my daughter, and my mother back from the dead. The drunk driver who caused their death does not have a chance to retrieve that day and decide to live it differently. I no longer have a chance to be a better husband to Lynda, father to Diana Jane, and son to my mother. I must live with the snapshot of the relationships as they were at the time of their death. I cannot change them now.

Regret is inescapable in a world of imperfection, failure, and loss. But can there also be redemption? Can a life gone wrong because of loss be made right again, however irreversible the loss itself? Can people with regrets be set free and transformed? I believe that there can be redemption, but only under one significant condition: *People* with regrets can be redeemed, but they cannot reverse the *loss* that gave rise to the regrets. People can be changed by the unchangeable losses they experience. Thus, for redemption to occur, they must let go of the loss itself and embrace the good effects that the loss can have on their lives. They must somehow transcend what lies behind and reach forward to what lies ahead, directing their energies toward changes they can make now. In other words, they must seek *personal transformation*, which comes only through grace.

I enjoyed a healthy, vital relationship with Lynda. We married young—I was twenty-one, she was twenty-two—and we helped each other grow up. We matured into adulthood together. Still, I could have been a better husband. I did not always champion her career aspirations and take her professional goals as seriously as I took my own. Both of us could have been better parents, too. We spanked too much, yelled too much, and did too much for our children. Sometimes we tried too hard to be the perfect family.

If I want transformation, I must let go of my regrets over what could have been and pursue what can be. But what I cannot have is the best of both worlds: the growth that has transformed my life as a result of the tragedy *and* the people whose death engendered that growth. There is a bitter irony here that cannot be avoided, however much we grow through loss. The people whose death enabled me to change for the better are the very people with whom I would most like to share these changes. Their death has forced me to grow; I wish now that they could benefit from the growth that has resulted from their death.

Many people are destroyed by loss because, learning what they could have been but failed to be, they choose to wallow in guilt and regret, to become bitter in spirit, or to fall into despair. While nothing they can do will reverse the loss, it is not true that there is nothing they can do to change. The difference between despair and hope, bitterness and forgiveness, hatred and love, and stagnation and vitality lies in the decisions we make about what to do in the face of regrets over an unchangeable and painful past. We cannot change the situation, but we can allow the situation to change us. We exacerbate our suffering needlessly when we allow one loss to lead to another. That causes gradual destruction of the soul.

This destruction of the soul represents the tragedy of what I call the "second death," and it can be a worse tragedy than the first. The death that comes through loss of spouse, children, parents, health, job, marriage, childhood, or any other kind is not the worst kind of death there is. Worse still is the *death of the spirit*, the death that comes through guilt, regret, bitterness, hatred, immorality, and despair. The first kind of death happens *to* us; the second kind of death happens *in* us. It is a death we bring upon ourselves if we refuse to be transformed by the first death.

Those who suffer loss face the temptation of confusing the two, of allowing the first death to justify the second. Still, these two deaths are not the same, however closely associated they seem to be. The first and more obvious death leads to but does not cause the second. It is like bad weather that deceives a farmer into thinking that his bad crop is the result of the weather rather than his decision to plant late or to put off the tilling. Thus a spouse's terminal illness may tempt us to despair of ever becoming a joyful person again; but the despair itself is not the result of the illness but of our attitude about it. Divorce may tempt us to hate an ex-spouse; but the hatred itself is not the result of the divorce but of the way we choose to respond to the divorce. Death of a child may tempt us to become self-pitying; but self-pity is not the result of the death but of a decision we make about the death. Chronic unemployment may tempt us to go on a binge; but the binge itself is not the result of the unemployment but of an unhealthy response to it.

It is natural, of course, for those who suffer catastrophic loss to feel destructive emotions like hatred, bitterness, despair, and cynicism. These emotions may threaten to dominate anyone who suffers tragedy and lives with regret. We may have to struggle against them for a long time, and that will not be easy. Few people who suffer loss are spared the temptation of taking revenge, wallowing in self-pity, or scoffing at life. But after a period of struggle, which sometimes leads to catharsis and release, it may become apparent to us that we are becoming prisoners to these emotions and captive to their power over our lives. At that point we must decide whether or not to *allow* these destructive emotions to conquer us. A bad choice will lead to the soul's death—a worse death by far than the death of a loved one or the job or one's health.

This struggle will show us that emotions like anger or self-pity, however natural and legitimate, do not define reality. Our feelings do not determine what is real, though the feelings themselves are real. We cannot ignore these feelings, but neither should we indulge them. Instead, we should acknowledge them without treating them as if they were ultimate truth. The feeling self is not the center of reality. God is the center of reality. To surrender to God, however contrary to our emotions, will lead to liberation from self and will open us to a world that is much bigger and grander than we are.

I met a woman recently whose presence made me weep even before we exchanged one word. She communicated profound depth, compassion, and grace to me. Something about her broke down my defenses. Later I found out why. She had lost two children at birth and an eleven-year-old daughter to cancer. She had suffered loss but had chosen nevertheless to embrace life. She became an extraordinary human being. I have also known people whose losses destroyed them. It is not that they suffered more than anyone else, or that they had to struggle more than anyone else. As I have already outlined, suffering and struggle are normal and even healthy. It is that their losses had turned them sour. Like everyone else, they faced the temptation of self-pity, bitterness, revenge, and all the rest. At that point they did not face these emotions squarely, acknowledge them for what they were, and seek to transcend them. They let their emotions determine what reality was for them. Consequently, they were not transformed by their suffering.

Regret can also lead to transformation if we view loss as an opportunity to take inventory of our lives. Loss forces us to see ourselves for what we are. For about four months after the accident I spent a great deal of time reviewing the quality of the marriage relationship I had with Lynda. Most of what I reviewed pleased me, though not all. I also explored my family history and observed patterns in my past that kept repeating themselves from one generation to the next. I looked hard at the kind of person I was. I kept asking questions and evaluating. I gained insights that were troubling to me. I saw how manipulative and self-righteous I was and how often I tried to impress and win others. This period of reflection proved to be liberating for me. I am more free from the past now than I would otherwise have been. Yet this freedom did not come from denying the past but from looking at it squarely, taking ownership of it, and allowing myself to be transformed by it.

My cousin Leanna, whose story I told in a previous chapter, has described to me the period of soul-searching that followed after discovering she had cancer. The knowledge of her own mortality, until then an abstract idea, made her take stock of her life. She was not entirely pleased with what she learned. She questioned the decision she had made to be a stay-at-home mother, and she wished she had pursued a career. But she also regretted not being a more attentive mother and wife. She reflected on her family background and the role it had played in shaping her character and values. She observed patterns of behavior in herself that fell short of the kind of person she wanted to be. This period of self-examination was both demanding and rewarding. It made her aware of her failures, but it also awakened her to new possibilities. It convicted her of guilt but also led her to grace. The fruit of her soul-searching is obvious now in the depth of character and faith she exhibits.

Failure to take stock almost ensures that we will repeat patterns that became chiseled into our lives before we suffered the loss. We will be inclined to remarry unwisely because we did not learn why we married unwisely the first time around. We will fall into the same addictions that led to the loss that so devastated our lives. We will continue to squander our resources because we refused to adopt the discipline we should have adopted much earlier. I know one woman whose failed marriage caused her to ponder why she had married her husband in the first place. That innocent question led her into a therapist's office, which was the turning point of her life. What she learned was unpleasant; what came out of it was wonderful.

Loss can also be transformative if we set a new course for our lives. My loss reinforced much of what I already believed; it confirmed that I was headed in the right direction. Still, I realized over time that I was too ambitious at work and too selfish at home. Loss broke me of some of those bad habits and also turned me toward my children. I had been attentive to them before, but since the accident I have begun to carry them in my heart. I once *performed* as a parent; now I *am* a parent.

A widow told me recently that the death of her husband caused her to reconsider her view of friendship. She said that she and her husband had always been best friends. She therefore had little time and interest to build friendships with others, including women. After her husband died, she began to view friendship through the eyes of one who needed it instead of one who was supposed to offer it. She realized she had dismissed friendships because her husband was friend enough; she never thought to befriend others for their sake, if not for her own. Her loneliness and isolation forced her to see life from another point of view. She gradually formed other friendships, and she was grateful that not everyone was as exclusive and inaccessible as she had been.

Finally, loss can be transformative if it causes us to seek the forgiveness of God. Sometimes the stalled motion picture reminds us of how far short we fell prior to the loss and how poorly we responded to it. The snapshot exposes our inner selves. We are forced to face the ugliness, selfishness, and meanness of our own lives. Then what? In this case, there are no second chances. We are left only with the bitter memory of our failures or even of the good intentions we had but failed to live up to. But God promises to forgive those of us who confess our failures, to absolve those of us who confess our guilt, and to make right what we are sorry for doing wrong.

The gift of divine forgiveness will help us to forgive ourselves. Without it, regret becomes a form of self-punishment. We see the evil we have done and the pain we have inflicted on others. We feel an acute sense of guilt. We loathe our selfishness and foolishness. And we know that there is nothing we can do to reverse the consequences of our actions. Yet a holy God imparts forgiveness if we sincerely ask for it; a just God shows us mercy and embraces us in love. If such a God can forgive us, then surely we can forgive ourselves. If such a God lavishes us with grace, then surely we can stop punishing ourselves and live in that grace. Divine forgiveness leads to self-forgiveness.

God's forgiveness will show us that he wants to take our losses and somehow bring them back upon us in the form of a blessing. This work of grace will not erase the loss or alter its consequences. Grace cannot change the moral order. What is bad will always be bad. But grace will bring good out of a bad situation; it will take an evil and somehow turn it into something that results in good. That is what God accomplished through the crucifixion. He turned the evil of an unjust murder into the good of salvation. God can do the same for us as well. We will not be delivered from suffering, but with God's help we can be transformed by it. The apostle Paul wrote that nothing can "separate us from the love of God that is in Christ Jesus our Lord."[1] Nothing! Not dangers, problems, conflicts, failures, guilt, regrets. Nothing. Not even our losses. That is the promise of true transformation; that is the power of the love of God.

I memorized that Pauline passage many years ago, and it came back to me after the accident. For months I felt shattered as a human being. I could do nothing for God and had little desire to obey him. Night after night I sat in my living room, unable to say anything, pray anything, or do anything. I was empty of energy and desire. All I could do was *let God love me*, even though I hardly believed that he loved anyone, least of all me. I had no idea how I could really believe or whether I even wanted to. I had no will or desire for it. But somehow I believed that not even my weakness of faith bothered God much. God loved me in my misery; God loved me because I was miserable. I learned through that experience that nothing can separate us from his love—not even our inability to love him in return! That was the first time in my life that I experienced the unconditional love of God.

Still, a problem remained. God may have promised forgiveness and unconditional love. But I wondered if I could trust a God who allowed, or caused, suffering in the first place. My loss made God seem distant and unfriendly, as if he lacked the power or the desire to prevent or deliver me from suffering. Though I believed that my transformation depended upon the grace of God, I was not sure I could trust this God. Was it even possible to believe in God, considering what had happened? As we shall see, that question haunted me for a long time.

The Terror of Randomness

Affliction is anonymous . . . ; it deprives its victims of their personality and makes them into things. It is indifferent; and it is the coldness of this indifference—a metallic coldness—that freezes all those it touches right to the depths of their souls. They will never find warmth again. They will never believe any more that they are anyone.

SIMONE WEIL

I remember having a conversation with Lynda once about an accident reported in our local newspaper. A station wagon with six children and their mother had skidded off the freeway, plunged down an embankment, and sunk in six feet of water. Three of the six children were killed. We both commented nervously that the problem was not simply that something bad had happened to innocent people—which struck us as bad enough—but that something bad had happened so randomly—which struck us as even worse. "Why did the tire blow out then and there?" we asked ourselves. We shivered with fear before the disorderliness of tragedy. If there was to be suffering, we at least wanted reason for it, predictability to it, and preparation to endure it. The randomness terrified us.

I remember the conversation with bitter irony now. For the last few years my predominant emotion has been a nervous and doleful bewilderment. Why, I have repeatedly asked myself, did it happen to us? Why were we at just that place, at just that time, under just those circumstances? Even a pause at a stop sign, a last-minute switch of seats before departure, a slower or faster rate of acceleration after a turn would have spared us all unspeakable suffering.

I have talked with Vietnam veterans who mention this same nervousness in the face of random suffering. One of them described walking on patrol with a fellow soldier who suddenly stepped on a land mine. The explosion killed his partner instantly. Another puzzled over the arbitrariness of death on the battlefield. The soldier to your right is wounded, the one to your left is killed, and you come out without a scratch.

Recently, a man who had been released from the Air Force because of mental health problems returned to his old base outside Spokane to hunt down the military psychiatrist who had recommended his discharge. The man found the psychiatrist in his office and shot him dead right in front of a patient. He then walked out of that office and down the hallway of the hospital, shooting people randomly. He killed three other people and wounded twenty-three before a military policeman gunned him down. His victims were all innocent bystanders who had no idea who this man was or why he was shooting. They were in the wrong place at the wrong time.

In that rampage, all four members of one family were wounded, the parents critically. Two small children, friends of that family, had accompanied them for the day; one of them, only eight years old, was killed. Her parents will feel both guilty and angry, I am sure. They will blame themselves for allowing her to go or blame the family for asking her to come. They will also feel rage toward the killer for doing such a senseless deed, especially to innocent people. But eventually they too will look dumbfounded at the utter randomness of it all. Why her? Why there? Why then? They will say, time and again, that it does not make sense. And they will be right to say it.

There is, of course, an orderliness to life. Nature reflects an orderliness that scientists observe and count on every day, or else they would not be able to do their research. Drop an object and it will fall toward earth at a constant rate of speed, as Newton discovered. Humans also impose order on the world, as we see, for example, through clocks, schedules, and city planning. But order does not always prevail. A family lives comfortably for forty years in a midwestern town. Suddenly a tornado blows through and destroys their home, but leaves every other house on the block untouched. A middle-aged man eats a proper diet and exercises regularly for many years, but a lump in his neck prompts him to visit the doctor, who tells him that he has lymphoma. A woman enjoys years of a career, marriage, and motherhood. Then one day while jogging in a park she is raped by a stranger. Suddenly her world turns ugly, and she turns bitter. She wonders with regret why she was running through the park at just that time and why her assailant was waiting at just that place.

Loss makes the universe seem like a cold and unfriendly place, as if it were little more than trillions of atoms colliding together with no predictability, no design, and no reason to it. Life just happens, whether good or bad. Randomness mandates that we simply live as best we can, but in the end we must realize that what happens is often arbitrary. At such times the universe seems to make about as much sense as a little girl who thinks that her fleeting grudge against a brother is the reason why he got measles.

One of the worst aspects of my experience of loss has been this sense of sheer randomness. The event was completely outside my control—an "accident," as we say. The threat of "anomie," as Peter Berger has called this disorderliness, was and still is almost unbearable to me. For months after the accident I turned the events of that day over and over in my mind. I kept reliving the day, changing the schedule in some way so that the accident would not occur. I also searched for reasons. I blamed myself for being a selfish husband, an inattentive father, or an aloof son. I wondered if my family had been cursed. I entertained the idea that the accident was a demonic attack. I looked with cynicism on the absurdity of life. Maybe, I thought, there really is no God and no meaning to life. I resigned myself to misery and death, thereby yielding to its inexorability. These machinations of the mind tormented me because I could not discover any explanation that made sense of the tragedy. An answer to the "Why?" question eluded me.

Suffering may be at its fiercest when it is random, for we are then stripped of even the cold comfort that comes when events, however cruel, occur for a reason. To fall while attempting a dangerous climb without ropes leads to one kind of suffering. We shake our heads at the tragedy but realize that the climber should have taken precautions or attempted a climb within his range of ability. What happened constitutes real suffering, but at least it is understandable. Sometimes people do jobs or hobbies that carry an inherent risk of injury or death. But to be killed by a random bolt of lightning or a stray bullet engenders another kind of suffering, in which case we tremble because there is no satisfactory explanation or no sensible pattern. Death just happened. The victim was simply at the wrong place at the wrong time.

The memory of one brief encounter that occurred right after the accident has stayed with me these several years because it illustrates so well this terror of randomness. After emergency crews arrived at the scene, I withdrew from trying to save the dying to find my children, who were being cared for by strangers. John was hysterical. We did not discover until later that the hysteria was caused by pain as well as fear, since he had broken his femur. I took him in my arms and began to walk away from the scene of chaos to calm him down. I had walked maybe fifty feet when I met a man with an obvious head injury staggering toward me. I sensed immediately that he was most likely the driver of the other car. Our eyes met briefly but intensely, as if both of us knew that something extraordinarily horrible had occurred between us. Then he lay down, and someone covered him with a blanket. I looked down at him for a moment as he lay there motionless at my feet, and he looked up at me. Though John was screaming, sirens were blaring, lights were flashing, and people were gaping from car windows, our eyes remained locked on each other. At that moment I thought to myself, *I don't even know this man. I may never see him again. Yet he has changed my life forever. What power he has over me and my children! He has killed three members of my family. How can this be?* Suddenly I felt the terror of randomness.

For a long time I wanted to change the events of that day so that I could alter the future that the accident had thrust upon me. I spent weeks imagining how I could rearrange the schedule so that we would not have to go to the powwow. Having exhausted that option, I pretended to stay longer at the powwow. I sent the children to the bathroom before driving home. I imagined taking a wrong turn or lingering longer at an intersection. I tried hard to alter in my imagination what had happened in reality.

But my brother-in-law Jack challenged me to reconsider whether I really wanted that kind of power. He said that life in this world is an accident waiting to happen, and there is not much we can do about it. Common sense, of course, tells us to wear seatbelts, drive the speed limit, eat healthy food, exercise regularly, get sufficient rest, and make wise decisions. These good habits will minimize accidents but not eliminate them. Did I really want to know what was going to happen in the future so that I could protect myself from the accidents that inevitably and randomly occur in every person's life? And if I knew what accidents were looming ahead and could change the course of my life, would I then want to know what accidents would befall me as a result of the new course I had set for myself? What I really wanted, he said, was to be God—an option obviously closed to me. So, if I really wanted to protect myself from accidents, he continued, I should lock myself inside an antiseptic bubble and live there for the rest of my life. But who would want that? Better, he concluded, to brace myself for accidents and endure them as best I can. Better to give up my quest for control and live in hope.

Maybe that is why most people seem to weather loss so well. They learn to live in hope. It is a wonder, considering the suffering that awaits us all, how few of us live in constant dread, utterly immobilized by what may happen to us. Somehow we manage to live reasonably well, expecting the best and, when the time comes to face the worst, accepting it as part of the bargain of living in a fallen world. We are remarkably resilient creatures. When knocked down, most of us get up, like weeds bouncing back after being trampled. We love again, work again, and hope again. We think it is worth the risk and trouble to live in the world, though terrors surely await us, and we take our chances that, all things considered, life is still worth living.

Life is indeed worth living to me, though it took me a long while to come to that conclusion. I was helped along the way by two stories in the Bible that gave me a new perspective on the terror of randomness. Both show how events that seem random may not be as capricious as we think. The first story, about a rich man named Job, explores the power we have to choose for God, though God appears distant and chaos seems to rule. The second story, about Joseph, demonstrates that God is in control, even when it is not obvious in our immediate experience.

At first the story of Job repulsed me.[1] I was finally forced to ponder it in depth in preparation for a lecture I had to give on Jewish views of suffering. The story begins by describing Job's prosperity and virtue. He is rich, has many children and a faithful wife, and is kind and generous. If there were a man alive who deserves such abundance, surely it is righteous Job. Then the story changes scenes. In the heavenly court Satan approaches God, who points to Job and says that no one is like him in faith and virtue. But Satan challenges God, arguing that Job is such a good and God-fearing man because God has made life easy for him. If God were to make life miserable for Job, God would see another side to him.

So Satan proposes a contest to see if Job will remain a righteous man in suffering. God accepts the challenge and gives Satan permission to make life hard for Job. Satan first takes away Job's wealth, then his children and servants, and finally his health. Job is left with nothing. He makes his way to an ash heap, where he scratches his sores and laments his fate. He is not privy, of course, to the contest in heaven between God and Satan; all he knows is his loss, pain, and misery.

The longest section of the story consists of a conversation between Job and three of his friends. These friends visit Job to comfort him. For seven days they sit with him in silence, so horrified by his appearance and suffering that they cannot speak. Finally, they venture to explain why Job has suffered such tragedy. They are all convinced that people like Job suffer because they deserve it. Though Job appears to be a good man, he must really be evil or else he would not be forced to face this calamity. Job cries out in despair and agony, complains to God, curses the day he was born, and wishes he were dead. But he does not curse God, nor does he accept the explanation of his three friends. He is no worse than other men, he says. In fact, he may even be better. Why, then, is he suffering so much more than everyone else? He can make no sense of it. His suffering seems random, and he is terrified by it.

Another character, Elihu, then steps forward. He has listened patiently to the conversation between Job and his three friends, and now it is his turn to speak. He raises questions about each of their perspectives and then offers another. He affirms that God is transcendent, despite what has happened to Job. He suggests that God speaks in mysterious ways—for example, in dreams—to communicate what people need to know, but have difficulty understanding, about God.

Finally, God appears to Job in a whirlwind and asks him a series of rhetorical questions, intended to show that he is transcendent, powerful, and wise, far superior to puny Job. "Can you cast the stars in space?" God asks Job. "Were you there at the creation of the world?" In the end Job admits he has spoken of matters he failed to understand. Amazing as it may seem, Job actually apologizes to God. Then God lifts him up, restoring everything twofold, and commands Job's three misguided friends to ask Job to pray for them, since they are at greater fault than Job.

When I first read this story, I was bothered by God's apparent injustice. Job seemed a pawn, his life subject to forces beyond his knowledge and control. I was also troubled by God's intimidating display of power, which seemed to bully Job into withdrawing his legitimate questions. As I discovered, however, I was critical of this story because I had been standing *outside* Job's experience and looking in, as if I were a research scientist observing subjects in a clinical experiment.

Job's story became more understandable and meaningful to me when I tried to stand *inside* his experience, which is possible for anyone who has suffered severe loss. I trembled before the power of Job's freedom to decide how he was going to respond to his suffering. How he exercised that freedom had repercussions even in God's heavenly court, where the hosts of heaven, including Almighty God, watched to see how Job's life would turn out. Job's choices really mattered to them. He had no idea how far his power reached, but he was not, as he was tempted to think, a solitary figure whose decisions counted for nothing.

I also realized that Job stopped asking questions not because God was a bully but because Job finally beheld God's unfathomable greatness in his immediate experience. He had spoken about God; then he came to know God. On meeting the real God, he simply had no more questions to ask. He discovered that God is the answer to all his questions, even questions he had not thought to ask. Job learned that behind the apparent randomness of life is the existence of God, whose greatness transcended Job but did not nullify the importance of Job's choices. Job ultimately found meaning in the ineffable presence of God, which he could not fully comprehend with his intellect but could only experience in the depths of his being.

The second story, about Joseph's experience of suffering, runs along two lines that eventually meet.[2] The first describes Joseph's suffering and eventual vindication. He is a favored and spoiled son. In a jealous rage his older brothers betray him. They sell him as a slave to some traders going to Egypt and tell their father Jacob that he was killed by a wild animal. In his first few years in Egypt, Joseph serves a wealthy and powerful leader, rising in his household until he assumes the highest position of authority. But again he is betrayed, this time by his master's wife. He is thrown in prison, where he rises to become the head of all prisoners. The storyteller asserts at two turning points in the plot that God is with Joseph, even in his suffering; and by the account of Joseph's behavior it is clear that Joseph believes it, though he has no apparent reason to. After interpreting a troubling dream that the king of Egypt had and advising him of a prudent course of action, Joseph is not only released from prison but is made the chief administrator of Egypt. He oversees the storage of surplus grain during seven years of plenty and the distribution of that grain during seven years of famine. After many years, Joseph's brothers travel to Egypt to buy grain. Joseph reveals himself to them (but only after testing them), and then moves their families and his father to Egypt, where they settle and prosper. That is the first story line.

But there is a second story line. It involves God's transcendent purpose, which makes Joseph's personal story a part of a much bigger story. Although Joseph suffers at the hands of his brothers, all the while God is planning to use Joseph's experience to move his family to Egypt, where they will live and eventually become slaves. Then, many years later, they will be led to freedom by Moses, one of the great leaders of the Jewish religion. Joseph has no idea that his story fits into this larger plot involving thousands of people and centuries of history. As it turns out, however, his life does not consist of a succession of isolated events randomly strung together but rather of a story with a purpose that he does not see and will never entirely understand.

Still, even within the limits of his lifetime Joseph understands enough to say to his brothers, "You intended to harm me, but God intended it for good. . . ."[3] Joseph acknowledges that great evil was done against him; but he also believes in the face of that evil that God's grace has triumphed over it. He recognizes in the unfolding of his life that God is good in ways that he could not see earlier. The Joseph story helps us to see that our own tragedies can be a very bad chapter in a very good book. The terror of randomness is enveloped by the mysterious purposes of God. In the end, life turns out to be good, although the journey to get there may be circuitous and difficult.

I have often imagined my own story fitting into some greater scheme, the half of which I may never fathom. I simply do not see the bigger picture, but I *choose to believe* that there is a bigger picture and that my loss is part of some wonderful story authored by God himself. Sometimes I wonder about how my own experience of loss will someday serve a greater purpose that I do not yet see or understand. My story may help to redeem a bad past, or it may bring about a better future. Perhaps my own family heritage has produced generations of absent and selfish fathers, and I have been given a chance to reverse that pattern. Perhaps people suffering catastrophic loss will someday look to our family for hope and inspiration. I do not know. Yet I choose to believe that God is working toward some ultimate purpose, even using my loss to that end.

Thornton Wilder suggests in *The Eighth Day* that we should understand our lives as a great landscape that extends far beyond what the eye of our experience can see. Who knows how one experience, so singularly horrible, can set in motion a chain of events that will bless future generations? Loss may appear to be random, but that does not mean it is. It may fit into a scheme that surpasses even what our imaginations dare to think.

Why Not Me?

Jean Valjean, my brother, you no longer belong to evil; but to good. It is your soul I am buying for you. I withdraw it from dark thoughts and from the spirit of perdition, and I give it to God!

VICTOR HUGO

I received many cards and letters after the accident. I am grateful that few people presumed to give advice. Instead, they expressed shock, anger, and doubt. "Why you?" they kept asking. As one person commented, "Your family appeared so ideal. This tragedy is a terrible injustice. If it can happen to you, it can happen to any of us. Now no one is safe!"

No one *is* safe, because the universe is hardly a safe place. It is often mean, unpredictable, and unjust. Loss has little to do with our notions of fairness. Some people live long and happily, though they deserve to suffer. Others endure one loss after another, though they deserve to be blessed. Loss is no more a respecter of persons and position than good fortune is. There is often no rhyme or reason to the misery of some and to the happiness of others.

Two weeks before the accident Lynda and I fell into a long conversation about what we would do if one of us were to die. We talked about how we would raise the children and what we would find most difficult about being single parents. We wondered which of our friends would remain loyal and which would drift away. We discussed money and time and home maintenance. The subject of remarriage came up too. We both agreed that under ideal conditions, having two parents in the home is best. But conditions are rarely ideal, which made us cautious about assuming we could find another spouse. We decided it would be better to remain single and pour energy into the children than to get involved in a relationship that would siphon energy from the home. Then Lynda cracked, "Besides, according to what I know about statistics, there would be no eligible men available to marry me. And according to what I know about you, there would be no women crazy enough to marry you!" In the end we felt a tremendous sense of relief that our conversation dealt in theory, not fact. We were glad we still had each other.

Why me? I have asked that question often, as many people do after suffering loss. Why did the loss happen to us? Why at such a young age? Why after trying so hard to keep the marriage together? Why in the prime of life? Why just before retirement?

Why me? Most of us want to have control of our lives. And we succeed a great deal of the time, which is due in part to the enviable powers we have at our disposal in Western civilization. We have access to good medical care, education, and entertainment. We have good jobs and comfortable homes. Consequently, we have the power to get much of what we want. But the possibility of so much control makes us vulnerable to disappointment when we lose it.

Loss deprives us of control. Cancer ravages, violence erupts, divorce devastates, unemployment frustrates, and death strikes—often with little warning. Suddenly we are forced to face our limitations squarely. Our expectations blow up in our face. We wonder what has gone wrong. We resent the intrusion, the inconvenience, the derailment. It is not something we were planning on! "Why me?" we ask.

I once heard someone ask the opposite question, "Why *not* me?" It was not a fatalistic question because he is not a fatalistic person. He asked it after his wife died of cancer. He said that suffering is simply a part of life. They had been married for thirty years, raised their children, served their community, and enjoyed many happy moments together. Then the time came to experience another side of life, the darker and more painful side. He could no more explain why his life had turned bad than he could explain why his life had been so good up to that point. Did he choose to grow up in a stable family? Did he have control over where he was born, when he was born, or to whom he was born? Did he determine his height, weight, intelligence, and appearance? Was he a better person than some baby born to a poor family in Bangladesh? He concluded that much of life seems just to happen; it is beyond our control. "Why *not* me?" is as good a question to ask as any.

This man has perspective. He understands his own loss in the light of global experience. The former Soviet Union lost nearly twenty million people during World War II, and that on top of the millions Stalin had exterminated in the 1930s. Virtually every family was touched by death. Europe lost a quarter of its population during the first phase of the Black Death from 1347–50. Hundreds of millions of people in the Third World live under conditions of such deprivation that they rarely see prosperity, to say nothing of experience it. They hardly know what they are missing. Youth growing up in many inner cities witness violence and drug addiction so often that it is as common to them as green lawns and friendly neighbors are to most of us who live in the suburbs. Millions of people endure abuse of one kind or another. "Why me?" seems to be the wrong question to ask. "Why *not* me?" is closer to the mark, once we consider how most people live.

I realized soon after the accident that I had just been initiated into a fellowship of suffering that spans the world. My tragedy introduced me to a side of life that most people around the world know all too well. Even now I hardly qualify, considering the good life I have been privileged to live for so many years and live even today. I still have a great deal of control. I belong to a wonderful community of people. I can afford a part-time nanny. I have a secure job with flexible hours and good benefits. I have a good heritage from which to draw strength and wisdom. The accident was really a brief, albeit dramatic, interruption in an otherwise happy, secure, and prosperous life. I am still white, still male, still American, still middle-class, still rich, still employed, still established, still loved. To many people I am even heroic, which is ironic to me, since I have only done what people around the world have been doing for centuries—make the most of a bad situation. So why *not* me? Can I expect to live an entire lifetime free of disappointment and suffering? Free of loss and pain? The very expectation strikes me as not only unrealistic but also arrogant. God spare me from such a perfect life!

Why me? Most of us want life not only to be under our control but also to be fair. So when we suffer loss, we claim our right to justice and resent circumstances that get in the way. We demand to live in a society in which virtue is rewarded and vice punished, hard work succeeds and laziness fails, decency wins and meanness loses. We feel violated when life does not turn out that way, when we get what we do not deserve and do not get what we feel we do deserve.

I do not believe for a moment that in the accident I got what I deserved. I am not perfect and never will be, but I am certainly no worse and maybe even better than some other people who seem to have it all. The explanation that people suffer or prosper according to their merits is too simple, for it does not square with human experience. I know the mother of four children, a woman not yet forty, whose husband recently died in an airplane crash. She is the epitome of goodness, kindness, and honesty, as was her husband. What did she do to deserve such a loss? I know another woman, close to eighty, who neglected and abused her three children while they were growing up, divorced two men because she was sick of being married to them, smokes and drinks constantly, and yet has good health, financial security, and many friends. What has she done to deserve such blessing?

Eight months after the accident the alleged driver of the other car was tried in federal court on four counts of vehicular manslaughter. I was issued a subpoena to be a witness for the prosecution, which meant that once again I had to face the man whom I had met on the road shortly after the accident. I dreaded this trip to Boise, where the trial was held. I was so nervous I actually got sick. I did not want revenge, but I did want justice so that the man whom I considered responsible for the deaths of four people would pay the just penalty for his wrongdoing. At least then there would be some vindication for the suffering he had caused.

The prosecution was confident of victory. The case seemed so obvious. But the defense attorney argued that no one could actually prove that the accused had been driving the car, since both he and his wife had been thrown from the vehicle. So the burden of proof was put on the prosecution. A witness saw the accused get into the driver's seat only ten minutes before the accident occurred. Other witnesses heard the accused admit after the accident that he had been the driver of the car. But the defense attorney was able to cast enough suspicion on the testimony of these witnesses to gain an acquittal for his client.

I was enraged after the trial, which in my mind turned out to be as unjust as the accident itself. The driver did not get what he deserved any more than the victims, whether living or dead, had gotten what they deserved. The travesty of the trial became a symbol for the unfairness of the accident itself. I had to work hard to fight off cynicism.

Yet over time I began to be bothered by this assumption that I had a right to complete fairness. Granted, I did not deserve to lose three members of my family. But then again, I am not sure I deserved to have them in the first place. Lynda was a woman of superior qualities, and she loved me through some very hard times. My mother lived well and served people to her life's end, and she showed a rare sensitivity to me during my rebellious teenage years. Diana Jane sparkled with enthusiasm for life and helped to fill our home with noise and excitement. Perhaps I did not deserve their deaths; but I did not deserve their presence in my life either. On the face of it, living in a perfectly fair world appeals to me. But deeper reflection makes me wonder. In such a world I might never experience tragedy; but neither would I experience grace, especially the grace God gave me in the form of the three wonderful people whom I lost.

I recently talked with a woman whose daughter was in an automobile accident. Her daughter, the driver of the car, was injured severely but survived, while the passenger in the car was killed. This woman agonized for her daughter, who feels guilty even though the accident was not her fault. Surprisingly, the mother feels guilty too. She does not understand why her daughter was spared while another mother's daughter was killed. She said to me, "The victim was not a worse person than my daughter. Her mother is not a worse mother than me. Why, then, did she die? Why does her mother have to suffer? It isn't fair. It doesn't make sense." Both mothers got what they did *not* deserve: the one's daughter was lost, the other's spared. But the mother of the survivor does not seem to be able to accept the grace that allowed her daughter to live. She feels guilty because she cannot accept something so undeserved. And it *was* undeserved, as undeserved as the other's death.

The problem of expecting to live in a perfectly fair world is that there is no grace in that world, for grace is grace *only when it is undeserved.* Victor Hugo's *Les Miserables* tells the story of Jean Valjean, who spends nineteen years in jail for stealing a loaf of bread and then for trying to escape his imprisonment. His sentence and suffering are obviously undeserved, the result of living in an unjust society. His experience turns him into a brooding, bitter man. His bitterness only increases when he begins to suffer the ignominy of being an ex-convict in nineteenth-century French society, which rejects disreputable people like Valjean.

In desperation he seeks lodging one night at the home of a Catholic bishop, who treats him with genuine kindness, which Valjean sees only as an opportunity to exploit. In the middle of the night he steals most of the bishop's silver, but he is caught by the police as he tries to flee. When the police bring him back to the bishop's house for identification, they are surprised when the bishop hands two silver candlesticks to Valjean, implying that he had *given* the stolen silver to him, and says, "You forgot these." After dismissing the police, the bishop turns to Valjean and claims him for God. "I have bought your soul for God," he tells him. In that moment, by the bishop's act of mercy, Valjean's bitterness is broken.

The rest of the novel demonstrates the utter power of a redeemed life. Valjean has every reason to hate and exploit, since fate so often turns against him; yet he chooses the way of mercy, as the bishop had done. He raises an orphan who is entrusted to his care at her mother's death, spares the life of a parole officer who has spent fifteen years hunting him, and saves a young man, his future son-in-law, from death, though it almost costs him his own life. He fulfills his destiny with joy, returns good for evil wherever he goes, and then longingly enters heaven.

At first Valjean sought to get what he thought he deserved and raged with anger when he failed. He changed his mind, however, after his encounter with the merciful bishop, becoming a merciful person himself. He never got what he deserved, either way. His life was both miserable and good. His suffering was undeserved, but so was his redemption.

Like Valjean, I would prefer to take my chances living in a universe in which I get what I do not deserve—again, either way. That means that I will suffer loss, as I already have, but it also means I will receive mercy. Life will end up being far worse that it would have otherwise been; it will also end up being far better. I will have to endure the bad I do not deserve; I will also get the good I do not deserve. I dread experiencing undeserved pain, but it is worth it to me if I can also experience undeserved grace.

If I have learned anything over the past three years, it is that I desperately need and desire the grace of God. Grace has come to me in ways I did not expect. Friends have remained loyal and supportive, in spite of my struggles. Quietness, contentment, and simplicity have gradually found a place in the center of my soul, though I have never been busier. I go to bed at night grateful for the events of the day, which I try to review and reflect on until I fall asleep, and I wake up in the morning eager to begin a new day. My life is rich and productive, like Iowa farmland in late summer.

My children have become a constant source of joy to me, however demanding my role as a single parent. Almost every day I take a few moments to listen to them practice their instruments, play a game with them, shoot a few baskets, talk about the day, and read aloud to them. When they go to bed, I always follow them down to their rooms and tuck them in. And just before I crawl into bed, I sneak into their bedrooms and pray God's blessing upon them, a practice I learned from Lynda. For four years now I have coached David's soccer team, and I occasionally take Catherine out to dinner or a concert. John, my youngest, is my constant companion; friends call him my clone and shadow.

Despite the fact that I had been a Christian for many years before the accident, since then God has become a living reality to me as never before. My confidence in God is somehow quieter but stronger. I feel little pressure to impress God or prove myself to him; yet I want to serve him with all my heart and strength. My life is full of bounty, even as I continue to feel the pain of loss. Grace is transforming me, and it is wonderful. I have slowly learned where God belongs and have allowed him to assume that place—at the center of life rather than at the periphery.

So, God spare us a life of fairness! To live in a world with grace is better by far than to live in a world of absolute fairness. A fair world may make life nice for us, but only as nice as we are. We may get what we deserve, but I wonder how much that is and whether or not we would really be satisfied. A world with grace will give us more than we deserve. It will give us life, even in our suffering.

Forgive and Remember

And so I discovered that it is not on our forgiveness any more than on our goodness that the world's healing hinges, but on God's. When He tells us to love our enemies, He gives, along with the command, the love itself.

CORRIE TEN BOOM

Tragic and catastrophic loss is often the result of wrongdoing.

Some people suffer loss because other people commit acts of betrayal, unfaithfulness, or brutality. Just a few days ago a young woman living in Spokane was abducted, robbed, and murdered by two teenagers. They dumped her body on the side of the road as if it were litter. Then they drove away in her car. A television reporter interviewed them after they were arrested. Neither denied the crime, although each accused the other of pulling the trigger. One of the accused actually snickered on camera and boasted, "I don't like living by the rules. I like things my way." His brazenness enraged the victim's family and friends. Their loss was the evil consequence of a calamitous wrong done to an innocent person.

Other people suffer loss because someone blunders. Stupidity and incompetence can cause just as much suffering as wickedness and brutality. Recently the newspaper ran a series of articles about an Air Force pilot who is being court-martialed for shooting down two helicopters in Iraq that ended up being American helicopters carrying American personnel, all of whom died in the mishap of "friendly fire." The tragedy was the costly outcome of incompetence and error. Last week a house fire in Spokane claimed the life of a nine-year-old girl who was trapped in the basement. The fire was started by a boy playing with a lighter. Her death was the grim consequence of his foolishness.

Still other people suffer loss because someone callously plots to do evil and cares nothing about the consequences. A number of years ago a score of people living in a small midwestern town lost their life savings because a trusted friend, charged with the responsibility of investing their wealth, squandered it in a scam and lost everything. I received a Christmas card and gift last year from a woman who is scrambling to raise her four young children and make ends meet because her husband left them. He was sick of marriage and parenthood. He wanted his freedom, so he got out. She and the children are struggling because his desire for independence was more important to him than their security and happiness. He *chose* divorce; it did not simply happen.

These losses are not random, like a freak accident or the occurrence of a natural disaster. They are the consequence of the malicious, foolish, or incompetent behavior of people who could have and should have behaved differently. Doctors blunder, investors turn greedy, neighbors exploit, relatives abuse, strangers rob and murder, drunk drivers speed and kill. Individual people make destructive choices that have devastating consequences for others as well as for themselves.

Most victims of wrongdoing want justice to prevail after their loss, and for good reason. They know intuitively that there is a moral order in the universe. The violation of that moral order demands justice. Without it, the moral order itself is undermined, simple rights and wrongs are made irrelevant, and people are given license to do whatever they want. Anything becomes possible and permissible. People who have suffered loss recoil before such an idea. They have become the victims of someone else's wrongdoing. Their undeserved, irreversible loss reminds them every day that wrong was done and that wrong must be made right, punishment meted out, the score evened, and restitution offered.

After the accident there was no question in my mind that a terrible wrong had been done to me and my family. On the way to the hospital I kept asking, "How could that driver have done such a thing?" Within a few days I was contacted by Idaho law-enforcement officials and later by a federal prosecutor. After the interviews and investigation the prosecuting attorney assumed that her office had enough evidence to convict the accused driver.

Everyone involved in the case was certain that the alleged driver of the other car was guilty. That certainty, as it turned out, made them overconfident. They did not take the investigation seriously enough, so they did not build a case that would have made conviction more likely. Confidence replaced competence. At the trial eight months later, as I have already recounted, the prosecution's case could not overcome the adroit arguments that the defense put forward. In the end it seemed that justice did not prevail.

I did not assume that conviction would come easily, nor that it was necessary for my own healing. I did not need to have the driver of the other car convicted, though I certainly wanted him to be. I realized our system of justice does fail. Sometimes the innocent are convicted and the guilty acquitted. I tried to distance myself from the trial so that my own sense of well-being would not depend on the trial's outcome. Still, I was not prepared for the disappointment I felt when the accused was acquitted.

During the months that followed the trial I thought often about the driver of the other car. I fantasized reading reports in the newspaper that he had died hideously or that he had committed a crime that put him behind bars for life. I wanted to see him suffer and pay for the wrong I believed he had done. I even dreamed of being in another accident with him. His car collided with mine. It was clearly his fault, as I believed it was the first time. But on this occasion a crowd of hundreds witnessed the accident and volunteered to testify against him.

It eventually occurred to me that this preoccupation was poisoning me. It signaled that I wanted more than justice. I wanted *revenge*. I was beginning to harbor hatred in my heart. I was edging toward becoming an unforgiving person and using what appeared to be the failure of the judicial system to justify my unforgiveness. I wanted to punish the wrongdoer and get even. The very thought of forgiveness seemed abhorrent to me. I realized at that moment that I had to forgive. If not, I would be consumed by my own unforgiveness.

Justice is not always served. Bad people get away with doing bad things. Rapists are not caught or convicted, abusive parents intimidate their children into silence, unfaithful spouses find happiness after the divorce, and greedy people force honest people into bankruptcy or ruin their reputation. If we insist life be fair, we will be disappointed. People will fail us and will not pay for it. Systems will fail us and will successfully resist efforts to reform them. Then what will we do?

Justice, of course, does not always fail. It often does its job, punishing wrongdoers. Yet strangely enough, even when justice does prevail, victims are not always satisfied. A just conclusion to a terrible injustice can actually lead to disappointment and depression, because sometimes victims want more than justice. They want the wrongdoer to hurt as much as they do, in the same way they do, and for as long as they do. A just outcome only reminds them that no punishment, however severe, can compensate for their loss and satiate their appetite for revenge. They still want to inflict pain on the person who did the wrong. The desire for revenge, therefore, is a bottomless pit. It cannot be satisfied, no matter how much revenge it gets.

The real problem, however, is not revenge itself but the *unforgiving heart* behind revenge. Unforgiveness is like fire that smolders in the belly, like smoke that smothers the soul. It is destructive because it is insidious. Occasionally it flares up in the form of bitter denunciation and explosions of rage. But most of the time it is content to stay low to the ground, where it goes unnoticed, quietly doing its deadly work.

Unforgiveness should not be confused with healthy responses to loss. The quest for justice, for example, reflects our belief in the moral nature of the universe. When wrong is done, we believe the wrongdoer should be punished. Anger, in turn, is a legitimate emotional response to suffering. When someone has done something hurtful to us, we want to strike back and hurt them. And grief is a natural condition that follows on the heels of loss. When we feel the absence of someone or something we lost, our soul cries out in anguish. These responses indicate that a normal person has just suffered loss and has begun the healthy but painful process of healing.

Unforgiveness is different from anger, grief, or the desire for justice. It is as ruinous as a plague. More destruction has been done from unforgiveness than from all the wrongdoing in the world that created the conditions for it. This destruction can occur on a large scale, as we see in Northern Ireland or in the Middle East. It can also occur on a small scale, as we observe in gang warfare, family feuds, and conflicts between former friends. In the name of unforgiveness people can do terrible things.

Unforgiveness uses victimization as an excuse. Unforgiving people become obsessed with the wrong done to them and are quick to say, "You don't know how unbearable my suffering has been! You don't know how much that person hurt me!" They are, of course, right. No one can know. But I wonder sometimes if being right is worth all that much. Is it worth the misery it causes? Is it worth living in bondage to unforgiveness? Is it worth the cycle of destruction it perpetrates?

There are visible signs of behavior that manifest an unforgiving heart underneath—signs alerting us to the problem and warning us that something bad is happening in our souls. Unforgiving people are quick to claim rights. They are sensitive to wrongs done to them, however slight, as if they had exposed nerves over their entire body. They are obsessed with the bad things that have happened to them in the past, and they are convinced that their circumstances are worse than everyone else's. They even gain pleasure in being victims. They actually enjoy their misery because it gives them a sense of power over their enemies, whom they blame for their problems, and power even over friends, to whom they complain and from whom they demand pity and understanding.

Unforgiveness is a temptation that most people who have suffered loss face. I think about Glen, whose failed marriage forced him to decide whether he would forever be a prisoner to his past or would learn to forgive the wrong done to him. Before telling me his story, Glen acknowledged that this was *his* story, told from *his* perspective. He did not want to give the impression that there was not another side to it.

Glen began by telling me about the distant past. He married young, shortly after both he and his future wife, Nancy, were converted to Christianity out of troubled backgrounds. After they were married Glen decided to attend a Bible school to prepare for the ministry. Nancy dutifully followed him. While there they had two children, became active in a church, and developed many friendships.

But Nancy grew restless and wanted to work outside the home. So she got a job at a newspaper. Soon Glen started hearing rumors of her flirtatious behavior at work. He was also startled when she invited a male coworker over for dinner, and the man began to lavish Nancy with gifts and attention. As other alarming signs followed, Glen became increasingly suspicious.

Several months later Nancy claimed that a close friend from another city had suddenly died. She wanted to go to the funeral, which was still three days away. That night she did not return home from work. She simply disappeared without a trace. By the third day following her disappearance, Glen was in a panic. He called Nancy's mother, who said that she knew nothing about such a friend. Then he called Nancy's office. Her supervisor said that she had not missed a day of work.

Nancy finally returned home six days later. She told Glen that she wanted out of the marriage and that if he refused, she would make him hate her. Then she assured him that he need not worry about losing his *entire* family: "Don't worry, I won't take the children from you."

Glen tried to appease her. He suggested that they move away and start over. He wondered if she needed space. Nancy consented to giving it a little time. She found an apartment so that she could live alone for a while. But a month later Glen discovered that she was living with another man. That was the final blow. He packed the family's belongings and moved back to his hometown, taking his children with him.

Still, hope lingered. Just before Glen's move he gave Nancy six months to make up her mind. When they met six months later, he asked, "Are you coming home?" Her answer was a simple "No." At that point Glen had no fight left, no hope left. So he consented to the divorce.

At first it did not even occur to Glen that he should forgive Nancy. He was too overcome by grief. But three experiences forced him to face her wrongdoing, his bitterness, and the need for forgiveness. The first was the utter shame he felt when he returned to his hometown. Three years earlier he had left his church a hero. His was a wonderful story of troublemaker turned saint and minister. Now he could no longer face the people who had sent him off to Bible college so hopefully. So he avoided everyone, even his closest friends.

The second experience occurred when the time came for Glen to send his children to visit their mother after a year's separation. The court had given him custody and Nancy visiting rights. She was allowed to have the children for one month during the summer. That arrangement seemed reasonable enough to Glen until the time came for them to leave. Then he remembered her promise, "I will never take the kids from you." Yet here she was, taking his children from him. He was miserable, and so were his children. He felt guilty that he was allowing his children to be exposed to a way of life he considered reprehensible. It was during that lonely month, while his children were away, that he began to want to punish Nancy for the pain she had brought into his life.

It was the third experience, however, that forced him to face his unforgiveness. Glen thought of himself as a spiritual man who had handled his wife's unfaithfulness and the divorce quite well. But some of his friends did not see it that way. Finally a pastor friend confronted him. He told Glen that he was pushing people away. He said that Glen's attitude was negative, especially when he talked about Nancy, and that he had begun to act like a victim. That one conversation, as painful as it was, made Glen see what was happening to his soul. He started to take inventory. He saw what he was doing to himself, to his children, and to his friendships. He wrestled with God. Finally he decided to forgive.

But forgiveness did not come easily or quickly. It was, as Glen now says, a process. He wanted to forgive, but it took time before he could actually forgive. The first step was identifying how Nancy had wronged him. He had to hold her responsible for breaking promises and for failing in her duty, both as a wife and as a mother. But he also had to see how negative he had become. He saw the bitterness that had taken root in his soul, and he wanted that bitterness uprooted. So he tried to change, in both attitude and behavior, and with God's help he succeeded. For example, he began to make positive comments about his former marriage. Later on he began to speak well of Nancy as she was, not as she once had been or as he wanted her to be. He finally began to wish her well and found that in wishing her well he became well himself. As he said to me, "My life was restored."

Glen discovered that unforgiveness simply continues the cycle of destruction that begins with the original wrongdoing. Unforgiveness does not stop the pain. It spreads it. Unforgiveness makes other people miserable, as Glen's friends told him. It fouls relationships with complaints, bitterness, selfishness, and revenge. Ironically, unforgiveness makes unforgiving people the most miserable people of all, for they more than anyone else must live with the poisonous consequences of their unforgiveness. Unforgiving people always find justification for their unforgiveness, and it is understandable that they do. No one can understand the pain they have suffered, and no one can deliver them from it. But neither do unforgiving people understand the pain their unforgiveness inflicts on others.

The process of forgiveness begins when victims realize that nothing—not justice or revenge or anything else—can reverse the wrong done. Forgiveness cannot spare victims the consequences of the loss, nor can it recover the life they once had. Victims have no power to change the past. No one can bring the dead back to life or erase the horror of a rape or pay back squandered investments. In the case of catastrophic loss, what has happened is done. There is no going back.

But there can be going ahead. Victims can choose life instead of death. They can choose to stop the cycle of destruction and, in the wake of the wrong done, do what is right. Forgiveness is simply choosing to do the right thing. It heals instead of hurts, restores broken relationships, and substitutes love where there was hate. Though forgiveness appears to contradict what seems fair and right, forgiving people decide that they would rather live in a merciful universe than in a fair one, for their sake as much as for anyone else's. Life is mean enough as it is; they choose not to make it any meaner.

It was the brokenness of my children that reminded me every day that they had had their fill of suffering. I did not want to see them suffer anymore. I realized that my unforgiveness would only prolong their pain. I knew that they were watching me, whether deliberately or unknowingly, to see how I responded to the wrong done to us. If I was unforgiving, they would most likely be unforgiving. If I was obsessed with the wrong done to me, they would be too. If I lived like a victim for the rest of my life, they would probably do likewise. If I drove all mercy from my heart, they would probably follow my example. They, too, would insist on fairness and, when that failed them, as it surely would, they would want revenge. I did not want such a plague in my home. I did not want to raise bitter children. So I chose to forgive, for their sake as well as my own.

I know many others who have decided to forgive wrongdoers for similar reasons. Glen wanted to protect his children, as I did. He also wanted to be free from bitterness so that he could respond to the new opportunities he believed lay ahead of him. Several years after his divorce he met Becky. He saw her often since she was the first grade teacher of both his children. He eventually took an interest in her and later fell in love. Not long after that, they were married. He became free to love again because he had forgiven. The depth of their relationship now shows evidence of the depth of his healing. I recently read about a woman who has begun to visit the man who murdered her son and who is now serving a life sentence for his crime. She, too, wants to stop the cycle of revenge by making her life a force for good.

But forgiveness is costly. Forgiving people must give up the right to get even, a right that is not so easy to relinquish. They must show mercy when their human sensibilities tell them to punish. Not that a desire for justice is wrong. A person can both forgive and strive for justice. Wrong that is forgiven is still wrong done and must be punished. Mercy does not abrogate justice; it transcends it.

However difficult, forgiveness in the end brings freedom to the one who gives it. Forgiving people let God run the universe. They let God punish wrongdoers as he wills, and they let God show mercy as he wills too. That is what Job and Joseph came to, as we have already observed. That is also what Jesus decided, as demonstrated by the pardon he granted his accusers and executioners while dying on the cross.

I think that I was spared excessive preoccupation with revenge because I believe that God is just, even though the judicial system is not. Ultimately every human being will have to stand before God, and God will judge every person with wisdom and impartiality. Human systems may fail; God's justice does not. I also believe that God is merciful, in ways that far exceed what we could imagine or muster ourselves. It is the tension between God's justice and mercy that makes God so capable of dealing with wrongdoers. God is able to punish people without destroying them, and to forgive people without indulging them.

Forgiving people, therefore, define the role they play in life modestly. They simply let God be God so that they can be normal and happy human beings who learn to forgive. Rather than think that they must even all scores, make sure justice prevails, and punish all wrongs, they simply choose to live as responsibly and humbly as they can. They try to impart a little grace to people in need, most of whom are as broken as they are anyway, and they try to do what is right in the face of so much wrong. It occurred to me about a year after the accident that I would never want to trade places with the alleged driver of the other car, who, I assume, was either tormented by guilt or hardened to all feeling. My feeling of sorrow was bad enough in itself. I could not imagine feeling guilt on top of that. Yet a worse state still, far exceeding even sorrow or guilt, is the absence of all feeling, for that means that the soul is dead.

Forgiving people want God's mercy to win out. They want the world to be healed of its pain and delivered from the evil that threatens at every turn to destroy it utterly, including the evil that threatens to destroy their own souls. If healing requires forgiveness, then they are willing to forgive. They see that unforgiveness only makes the soul sicker and sicker. That kind of chronic sickness only increases the price they will have to pay to get well again.

Unforgiveness makes a person sick by projecting the same scene of pain into the soul day after day, as if it were a videotape that never stops. Every time the scene is replayed, he or she relives the pain and becomes angry and bitter all over again. That repetition pollutes the soul. Forgiveness requires that we refuse to play the videotape and choose to put it on the shelf. We remember the painful loss; we are aware of who is responsible. But we do not play it over and over again. Instead, we play other tapes that bring healing to us. Thus, forgiveness not only relieves an offender from guilt; it also heals us from our sickness of soul.

Forgiveness rarely happens in an instant. It took Glen time to forgive. The same was true for me. Forgiveness is more a process than an event, more a movement within the soul than an action on the surface, such as saying the words, "I forgive you." In one sense, forgiveness is a lifelong process, for victims of catastrophic wrong may spend a lifetime discovering the many dimensions of their loss. I have no vain notions that I have finally and forever forgiven the one who was responsible for the accident. I may have to forgive many times more—such as at the weddings of my children and at the births of my grandchildren, for these events will remind me not only of gracious gifts given but also of precious people taken away.

Though forgiveness may not have an ending, it has a beginning. It begins when victims identify the wrong done to them and feel the anger that naturally rises in the soul. They realize that what happened to them was inexcusable and should not have happened. Before victims can show mercy, in other words, they must claim justice. Before they can forgive, they must accuse.

Anything short of holding wrongdoers accountable for their actions is an insult to the wrongdoers themselves. It reduces them to something less than human, for one of the primary characteristics of being human is knowing what constitutes right and wrong and what it means to be responsible, whether one chooses to be or not. We do not have to forgive animals for killing other animals because they kill by instinct and for food. We do have to forgive people for killing other people because they kill by choice. To dismiss wrong done because it was done out of ignorance or sickness or a bad background is to violate the wrongdoer's humanity. The starting point of forgiveness, then, is a recognition that the person or persons who did the wrong were in fact wrong. They knew better and could have—even should have—done otherwise.

Forgiveness also has limitations. It cannot do everything necessary to make life perfect. That kind of power belongs only to God. It cannot absolve the wrongdoer of guilt, erase the natural consequences that follow wrongdoing (like a prison term), or make the wrongdoer right with God or society. But forgiveness has the power to cancel the consequences of the wrongdoing in the relationship between wrongdoer and victim. Forgiving people give up the right to punish and instead wish wrongdoers well, whether they are starting a new marriage after a divorce or a new life after serving time in prison or a new relationship with God. Forgiveness hopes that wrongdoers experience a good life, which is a life full of the mercy of God.

Forgiveness does not mean forgetting. Not only is forgetting impossible for most people, considering the enormity of suffering; it is also unhealthy. Our memory of the past is not neutral. It can poison us or heal us, depending upon *how* we remember it. Remembering the wrong done can make us a prisoner to pain and hatred, or it can make us the recipient of the grace, love, and healing power of God. The experience of loss does not have to leave us with the memory of a painful event that stands alone, like a towering monument that dominates the landscape of our lives. Loss can also leave us with the memory of a wonderful story. It can function as a catalyst that pushes us in a new direction, like a closed road that forces us to turn around and find another way to our destination. Who knows what we will discover and see along the way?

The suffering my children, family, friends, and I have experienced is part of an ongoing story that is still being written. I still remember the accident. Who could forget the horror of it? But I also remember what has happened since. Who would want to forget the wonder of that? My memory has become a source of healing for me. It reminds me of the loss. But it also tells me that the loss was not simply the ending of something good; it was also the beginning of something else. And that has turned out to be good, too.

In the end, I wonder whether it is really possible to forgive wrongdoers if we do not trust God first. Faith enables us to face wrongdoing in the light of God's sovereignty. Though unforgiveness was once a temptation to me (as it may be again in the future), it was not an insurmountable one. I knew that God was somehow in control. If I had anyone to turn to for help, it was God. Then again, if I had anyone to blame, it was also God. My belief in his sovereignty was not always a comfort to me, as we shall see in the next chapter. But it did focus my attention less on people, however terrible their wrongdoing, and more on God. I held God responsible for my circumstances. I placed my confidence in him; I also argued with him. In any case, God played the key role.

Faith also changes our attitude about the people who wrong us, for it forces us to view their wrongdoing in the light of our own. Knowledge of God reveals knowledge of ourselves as well. We learn that we bear the image of God, but we also see that we are sinful. Sinful people need God's forgiveness. Jesus once said that people who are forgiven much love much. The experience of forgiveness makes us forgiving. Once we see ourselves as people who need God's mercy, we will be more likely to show mercy to others.

As I look back now, I see that no matter where I turned after my loss, I kept running into God. I shivered before the randomness of my suffering. I asked, "Why me?" I wrestled with unforgiveness. The questions I asked, the temptations I faced, the revenge I sought, the bewilderment I felt, and the grief I experienced all pushed me inexorably toward God. If God really was God, where was he when the tragedy occurred? Why did he do nothing? How could God allow such a terrible thing to happen? My suffering, in short, forced me to address the problem of God's sovereignty.

The Absence of God

It is said of God that no one can behold his face and live. I always thought this meant that no one could see his splendor and live. A friend said perhaps it means that no one could see his sorrow and live. Or perhaps his sorrow is his splendor.

NICHOLAS WOLTERSTORFF

I have had a few close calls in my life. The memory of one in particular has remained with me all these years. I was twelve years old, and my family was staying for the summer in a trailer near Holland, Michigan. Our next door neighbors were close friends. They had an eighteen-year-old son, Dave, who was just a year older than my sister. One afternoon Dave asked me to ride along with two of his friends to pick up two of their sisters, who had been horseback riding. Of course I wanted to go. What boy my age would not want to go cruising with a carload of teenagers? But my dad and mom were in the middle of a tussle when I asked permission to go. My dad cut me off with a curt "no." In less than an hour all five of them were killed in a terrible accident.

I was only mildly religious at the time. Still, I remember feeling both frightened and relieved that God had spared me from such an untimely and horrible death—afraid because I had brushed death, and relieved because God, in his sovereignty, had preserved my life. Perhaps I was too young and egocentric to contemplate the tragedy from the victim's point of view. If God had spared me, did that mean that God had killed them? If I had ended up on the winning side of God's sovereignty, did that mean that they had ended up on the losing side?

I still believe that God is sovereign over time, space, and creation. He is in absolute control of everything that happens. The Hebrew word for the Divine Name, Yahweh, can be translated, "I am who I am," which means that God is the One who really is, God is ultimate reality, God is sovereign. God has complete authority in the universe.

God's sovereignty may follow logically from who God is by definition. It may even reflect our experience of God as the One who spares and blesses us. But this positive inclination toward God's sovereignty may come to a sudden stop in the face of severe loss. How, in such circumstances, can we reconcile God's sovereignty with human suffering, or God's control with our pain, especially if we believe that God is both good and powerful?

This question introduces us to the perennial problem of theodicy, which is humanity's attempt to reconcile the apparent contradiction between the experience of suffering and the existence of a good and powerful God. There appear to be two possible answers: Either God is powerful but not good, and thus a cruel God who causes suffering; or God is good but not powerful, and thus a weak God who cannot prevent suffering, though he would like to. Both answers have problems because they appear to undermine what we *want* to believe about God, namely, that he is both powerful *and* good.

I avoided even thinking about God's sovereignty after the accident. The very idea that the God whom I had tried for so many years to trust and follow would allow or even cause such a tragedy was unthinkable to me—as repugnant to my religious sensibilities as the death of my loved ones had been to my human sensibilities. But over time I realized that the trajectory of my grief had set me on a collision course with God and that eventually I would have to wrestle with this most complex of issues. I knew I had to make peace with God's sovereignty, reject God altogether, or settle for a lesser God who lacked the power or desire to prevent the accident.

My loss made God seem terrifying and inscrutable. For a long time I saw his sovereignty as a towering cliff in winter—icy, cold, and windswept. I stood in my misery at the base of this cliff and looked up at its forbidding, unscalable wall. I felt overwhelmed, intimidated, and crushed by its hugeness. There was nothing inviting or comforting about it. It loomed over me, completely oblivious to my presence and pain. It defied climbing; it mocked my puniness. I yelled at God to acknowledge my suffering and to take responsibility for it, but all I heard was the lonely echo of my own voice.

Such may be the impression that God's sovereignty leaves with those who have suffered a severe loss. It seems awful and inaccessible. We ask God, "Why have I suffered?" But God does not seem to hear or want to answer, as if we were too insignificant for a reply. We look to God for perspective, consolation, and deliverance, but do not receive any of these gifts of mercy. Instead, we face a granite wall that cannot—or will not—respond to our need and our cries. God may exist—transcendent, ubiquitous, and omniscient—but he does not seem to care about us. So we ask ourselves, "Who needs this kind of God?"

Perhaps, then, God does not exist at all. Suffering may push us far enough in the direction of doubt that we arrive at atheism. Perhaps God is a human invention, as Ludwig Feuerbach argued, a projection of humanity onto the cosmos. God then may be nothing more than a useful fiction that functions to explain our origins, make sense out of reality, and provide us with security in a vast, impersonal universe. But as our knowledge of the universe and our control over nature grows, our need for God diminishes.

At one time most people believed that God created the universe. Since Charles Darwin, more and more people believe that the universe is a product of random forces and natural selection. Likewise, at one time most people believed that God created the soul, which gave humans the capacity to know God. Since Sigmund Freud, a growing number of people believe that human nature is the product of unconscious drives and external environment. If God is a useful fiction, God appears to be getting less useful all the time. Eventually the growth of knowledge may make the existence of God seem entirely unnecessary.

Darwin, Freud, Feuerbach, and many other Western thinkers raised *intellectual* questions about God, challenging his very existence. These questions trouble many people and have driven some away from faith altogether. But suffering also raises *emotional* questions about God. God may or may not exist, but who wants a God who allows suffering, even though he could presumably do something about it, or who shrinks before suffering, lacking the power to alleviate it? It would almost seem better if God did not exist at all. Having no God may be preferable to having a weak or a cruel God.

This issue is not as abstract and speculative as it sounds, the business of intellectuals and no one else. Suffering does not allow us the luxury of keeping the question at a safe distance. Rather, suffering forces us to think about God's essential nature. Is God sovereign? Is God good? Can we trust him? After many years of infertility Lynda finally conceived, which was a miracle to us, since we had exhausted all the medical options open to us and had finally allowed our physician's discouraging prognosis to sink in. Lynda was already thirty-two, and she believed that this baby was probably going to be her only one. We therefore set to work immediately to prepare our home for a new infant and Lynda for delivery. She was overcome with joy.

But seven weeks later she miscarried. The miscarriage devastated her. She became profoundly sad and disillusioned, and for many months she was angry at God. She said to me once, "My earthly father would never do such a thing to me, but my heavenly Father has." It was the darkest hour of her life.

That struggle in her soul was only resolved by Catherine's birth a year and a half later. Lynda felt great sympathy for couples whose problems with infertility were not solved as satisfactorily as ours had been. That sympathy made her hesitate to turn the miraculous births of our four children into a sentimental testimony. She never wanted to exacerbate the silent sadness that so many infertile couples feel. She also realized that, though childlessness would have ultimately served some positive spiritual purpose in her life, she preferred the happy ending that came instead. As she said to me once, with a puckish grin on her face, "I wanted to be a mother more than I wanted to be a saint anyway."

The issue of God's sovereignty is no longer a mere abstraction to me either. I chose to become a professor because I *wanted* to think about big questions like this one, which have always fascinated me. But after the accident I *had* to think about them, especially about God's sovereignty, which forced itself upon me through the crisis of my experience. For years I had prayed every morning that God would protect my family from harm and danger, and I thanked God every night that these prayers had been answered. I did not thank God the night of the accident, and I hesitated for many months afterwards to begin praying again for anything. I was tortured by the question of where God was that night. I wondered whether I would ever again be able to trust him.

I longed to continue believing in God. It was bad enough to lose three members of my family. Why make things worse by losing God, too? I realized that he was the only foundation on which to build my broken life. Still, I could not help asking, "What if God—the God I have trusted for so long—does not exist?" I followed the trail of that question for a while, looking honestly at where it would lead me. Since suffering made belief in God more difficult, at least for a time, I decided to investigate the implications of unbelief. What would atheism do for me in my suffering that belief in God did not do or could not do?

The farther I followed the trail of this question, the more troubled I became. I discovered that sorrow itself needs the existence of God to validate it as a healthy and legitimate emotion. If there is no God, human emotion collapses into a terrible relativism, and it makes no difference how we respond to loss. It becomes entirely subjective, like individual tastes in ice cream. I cried at the funeral because I lost three people whom I loved. But why? Why not snicker at their burial and scoff at the whole experience? We grieve the dissolution of a marriage. But again, why? Why not celebrate the freedom from obligation and urge married people to take such commitments less seriously? We mourn a man's tragic accident and severe disability. But why not laugh at his condition instead? We empathize with a couple who has a Down's syndrome baby. But why not urge them to institutionalize the baby and try again?

If there were no God, there appears to be no ultimate reason why we should feel one way or the other, since emotions like grief or happiness have no grounding in a greater, objective reality outside the self. In an atheistic worldview, it becomes all but impossible to establish the absoluteness of truth and falsehood, or good and evil, or right and wrong. Hence, there seems to be no objective reason why we should view catastrophic loss as bad and why we should feel bad about it. Emotion, like human experience in general, seems relative. Not that atheists feel less bad about suffering than religious people do. Suffering hurts, no matter what the worldview of the people who experience it. It is the fact that we identify something as bad that makes me want to ask, "Where did we get the idea of good or bad in the first place?"

People feel pain in the soul for a reason. They *feel* bad in their suffering because the loss they suffered *is* bad. Tragic death is bad, betrayal in marriage is bad, sexual abuse is bad, terminal illness is bad, severe disability is bad. We know these losses are bad because we have knowledge of the good—not merely preferences or opinions or feelings, but knowledge. Such knowledge can only come from the existence of God.

I realize that other people who have suffered loss have come to different conclusions from mine, and they are just as sincere and serious as I am. Some believe that we know good and bad through the operation of natural law, which governs the moral universe in the same way it governs the physical universe. Others believe that we have knowledge of good and bad through the influence of social convention. But these options seem to beg the question. Where did natural law originate? What is the source of social convention? These questions push me away from atheism and toward God.

The implications of atheism are therefore intolerable to me. However difficult belief in God can sometimes be, belief in atheism is more difficult still. It deprives us of the objective view of reality we need to validate our feelings about the losses we suffer. Sorrow, anger, and depression—these are genuine expressions of a soul that has a valid reason to convulse. The soul suffers because bad has appeared to triumph over good. It is the existence of God that provides categories by which we make moral judgments and respond with appropriate emotions. We have good reason, then, to mourn our losses. Tears at a funeral, hospital, divorce court, or therapist's office manifest sadness in the face of legitimate loss. What we lost was good; what we lost rightfully makes us feel bad. The system of meaning that makes us feel bad about the loss—and gives us the *right* to feel bad—reflects a universe that has God at the center of it. There may be other explanations, but this one makes the most sense to me.

The trail of atheism I followed, therefore, led me right back to belief in God. But I still found myself bewildered by his sovereignty. It still towered over me like a huge, granite cliff. I have not yet found a simple explanation, nor am I sure I ever will or even want to. There is too much mystery to make God's ways easy to explain. Still, I keep circling this mystery, exploring it from a variety of perspectives. In the process, I have discovered three perspectives that have helped me.

The first perspective has to do with an alternative way of understanding God's sovereignty. Prior to the accident, I held a narrow view of his sovereignty, though I did not realize it at the time. I was inclined to believe that God simply pulled the strings and manipulated the events of our lives as if we were marionettes on a string and God was a puppeteer controlling us completely. Such a view is obviously deterministic, as if life happens to us as dictated by God. He sets the course, and we have to follow it. God is active and inflexible; we are passive victims. We have no meaningful choices, no real options, and no legitimate freedom. According to this view, we are more like puppets than people.

Since the accident I have begun to question this perspective. I have started to broaden my understanding of God's sovereignty so that it includes rather than nullifies human freedom. I have come to realize that I can affirm God's sovereignty and still be a person instead of a puppet. I believe now that my view of God's sovereignty was once far too small. His sovereignty encompasses all of life—for example, not simply tragic experiences but also our responses to them. It envelops all of human experience and integrates it into a greater whole. Even human freedom, then, becomes a dimension of God's sovereignty, as if God were a novelist who had invented characters so real that the decisions they make are genuinely their decisions. As the novelist, God stands outside the story and "controls" it as the writer. But as characters in the novel, humans are free to act and to determine their own destiny. God's sovereignty, then, transcends human freedom but does not nullify it. Both are real—only real in different ways and on different planes.

Belief in God's sovereignty thus gives us the security of knowing God is in control, but it also assigns us the responsibility of using our freedom to make wise choices and to remain faithful to him. It assures us that God is transcendent without canceling out the important role we play. God's sovereignty allows us to believe that he is bigger than our circumstances and will make our lives better through those circumstances.

The second perspective concerns the peculiar relationship that exists between God's sovereignty and the Incarnation. God's sovereignty means that God is in ultimate control of everything. The Incarnation means that God came into the world as a vulnerable human being. God was born to a woman, Mary. He was given a name, Jesus. He learned to walk and talk, read and write, swing a hammer and wash dishes. God embraced human experience and lived with all the ambiguities and struggles that characterize life on earth. In the end he became a victim of injustice and hatred, suffered horribly on the cross, and died an ignominious death. The sovereign God came in Jesus Christ to suffer with us and to suffer for us. He descended deeper into the pit than we will ever know. His sovereignty did not protect him from loss. If anything, it led him to suffer loss for our sake. God is therefore not simply some distant being who controls the world by a mysterious power. God came all the way to us and lived among us. The icy cliff became a pile of sand at our feet.

The God I know has experienced pain and therefore understands my pain. In Jesus I have felt God's tears, trembled before his death on the cross, and witnessed the redemptive power of his suffering. The Incarnation means that God cares so much that he chose to become human and suffer loss, though he never had to. I have grieved long and hard and intensely. But I have found comfort knowing that the sovereign God, who is in control of everything, is the same God who has experienced the pain I live with every day. No matter how deep the pit into which I descend, I keep finding God there. He is not aloof from my suffering but draws near to me when I suffer. He is vulnerable to pain, quick to shed tears, and acquainted with grief. God is a suffering Sovereign who feels the sorrow of the world.

The Incarnation has left a permanent imprint on me. For three years now I have cried at every communion service I have attended. I have not only brought my pain to God but also felt as never before the pain God suffered for me. I have mourned before God because I know that God has mourned, too. God understands suffering because God suffered.

The final perspective concerns the role of faith, which seems to be required of anyone who wants to know God. I have wondered for a long time why faith is so essential. Why did God not make his divine nature more obvious? Why did God not make it easier for us to believe? It seems to me that we know enough to believe but not so much that we are compelled to believe. The Bible points to the splendor of the world as evidence of God's existence, to certain episodes in history as proof of God's work in the world, and to the coming of Jesus to earth as the ultimate manifestation of his love for all of us. Yet it is possible to see the natural world in a way that excludes God, to view history as empty of divine involvement, and to interpret Jesus as simply a great moral teacher, a radical revolutionary, or a deranged fanatic. We can live normal and productive lives on earth and dismiss God. We can choose to be atheists and get away with it.

The point is that we have a *choice*. More than anything, God covets our love. But real love can never be forced. Freedom is what makes love possible in the first place. That is why God will never coerce us into a relationship. Faith allows us to choose God in freedom. It is possible to believe in him, but it is also possible *not to* believe in him. If we believe, it is because we have *chosen* to believe, although even the opportunity to make a choice is itself a divine gift.

Loss may call the existence of God into question. Pain seems to conceal him from us, making it hard for us to believe that there could be a God in the midst of our suffering. In our pain we are tempted to reject God, yet for some reason we hesitate to take that course of action. So we ponder and pray. We move toward God, then away from him. We wrestle in our souls to believe. Finally we choose God, and in the choosing we learn that he has already chosen us and has already been drawing us to him. We approach him in our freedom, having minds that can doubt as well as believe, hearts that can feel sorrow as well as joy, and wills that can choose against God as well as for him. We decide to be in a relationship with God. And then we discover that God, in his sovereignty, has already decided to be in a relationship with us.

In the end, however, I do not think that I will ever be able to comprehend God's sovereignty. The very idea transcends the mind's capacity to fathom it. Still, I have come to a partial resolution. I have made peace with his sovereignty and have found comfort in it. It is no longer odious to me. That peace came in the form of a waking dream. As I mentioned before, the memory of the accident was etched into my mind the moment it occurred. For a long time it was a source of torment to me. Then one night, as I lay sleepless in bed, I saw the accident in a new light. I was standing in a field with my three children, near the scene of the accident. The four of us were watching our minivan as it rounded that same curve. An oncoming car jumped its lane, just as it had in the accident, and collided with our van. We witnessed the violence, the pandemonium, and the death, just as we had experienced it in real life. Suddenly a beautiful light enveloped the scene. It illuminated everything. The light forced us to see in even greater detail the destruction of the accident. But it also enabled us to see the presence of God in that place. I knew in that moment that God was there at the accident. God was there to welcome our loved ones into heaven. God was there to comfort us. God was there to send those of us who survived in a new direction.

This waking dream did not give me an answer to the question of why the accident happened in the first place, nor did it convince me that it was good. It did not erase my grief or make me happy. But it did give me a measure of peace. From that point on I began, in small ways at least, to believe that God's sovereignty was a blessing and not a curse. The cliff still towers above me, but now it gives me security and fills me with awe.

Life Has the Final Word

The edges of God are tragedy. The depths of God are joy, beauty, resurrection, life. Resurrection answers crucifixion; life answers death.

MARJORIE HEWITT SUCHOCKI

After the funeral I tried to resume a normal routine in our home as quickly as possible. One aspect of that routine was evening Bible reading. About six weeks after the accident, the four of us sat down together on the sofa one night to read a story from the book of Acts—the story of Peter raising Dorcas from the dead. Immediately after the story Catherine blurted out, "Why didn't God do that for us? Why did God allow Mommy, Diana Jane, and Grandma to die? Why doesn't God care about us?" Her questions ignited all of them. They expressed rage at God for destroying our family, and they cried bitter tears. After tucking them into bed, I wandered over to a friend's house and cried as hard as they had.

That experience marked the first occasion when I learned the painful truth that I could not protect my children from suffering but could only go through it with them. It also marked the first occasion when I realized that the real enemy we faced—the last great enemy—was death. When I looked at them that night, I saw that they too would someday die, as their mother, sister, and grandmother had died. Of course I knew this truth before that night, but I came to know it on a deeper level. I felt the pall of death hanging over all of us.

We do not happily and willingly accept life's mortality, which is an affront to everything we cherish. We want to control how life will turn out and claim the good life for ourselves: successful careers, happy marriages, perfect children, close friends, beautiful homes, peaceful communities. Loss reminds us that we do not have the final word. Death does, whether it be the death of a spouse, a friendship, a marriage, a job, or our health. In the end death conquers all.

It is inevitable, then, that loss of any kind forces us to look hard and long at the reality of death. Does death really have the final word? Many people believe this grim truth to be the case. In the face of it, some choose to live heroically in spite of their destiny. Others choose to live only for the moment, giving themselves to every pleasure possible or securing as much power for themselves as they can. Still others see the absurdity of life and end it quickly by committing suicide.

Like anyone who suffers loss, I wanted to reverse my circumstances and bring my family members back to life again. The problem with this desire, however, is that eventually I would have lost my loved ones again. Lynda would have died another way, and who knows how horrible it might have been. My mother would have died again, perhaps suffering for years first. Diana Jane would surely have suffered in some way before going to the grave. We are deceived by our longings for what we once had, because we cannot have it that way forever, even if we regain what we lost for a while.

I have come to realize that the greatest enemy we face is death itself, which claims everyone and everything. No miracle can ultimately save us from it. A miracle is therefore only a temporary solution. We really need more than a miracle—we need a resurrection to make life eternally new. We long for a life in which death is finally and ultimately defeated.

Many religions contain stories that promise life after death. These stories are mythical but still meaningful, because they express the deepest longing of the human heart. To my knowledge, however, only one religion claims that an actual historical figure died and rose again, not as a resuscitated corpse destined to die again, but as a resurrected person destined to live eternally. That religion, of course, is Christianity. The historical figure is Jesus of Nazareth.

It is easy to be skeptical about the reliability of the stories that tell of Jesus' resurrection. They could be mere fabrications, dreamed up by his followers who respected and loved him so much that they did not want to let him go after he died. The resurrection could have been a convenient and creative way for them to keep him alive, though he really did die on the cross and never came to life again.

It was my own experience of tragedy and grief that gave me a different perspective on the resurrection accounts. My loss helped me to understand their loss. Loss leads to unrelenting pain, the kind of pain that forces us to acknowledge our mortal fate. It is possible, as we all know, to hold this terrible truth at bay for a while. Shock does that for us initially, which explains why people who lose a loved one or suffer some other kind of loss can be downcast one moment and euphoric the next, tearful one moment and giddy the next. But shock wears off over time. Then comes denial, bargaining, binges, and anger, which emerge and recede with various degrees of intensity. These methods of fighting pain may work for a time, but in the end they too, like shock, must yield to the greater power of death. Finally only deep sorrow and depression remain. The loss becomes what it really is, a reminder that death of some kind has conquered again. Death is always the victor.

But there is one notable exception. The followers of Jesus were devoted to him. They had sacrificed much to serve him. Suddenly their hero was gone. The account says that they became profoundly disillusioned by this turn of events and terrified that they, too, might die. So the disciples scattered like seeds in a gust of wind and hid from the Roman authorities in fear and bewilderment. The death of Jesus crushed them. They were no more ready to be joyful and courageous than I was after I saw my loved ones die in the accident. They could no more invent the idea of the resurrection in the weeks following his death than I could in my grief. They had no more energy and imagination to create a new religion than I did after suffering my tragedy. They could have tried—as I could have tried—but eventually their vain efforts would have failed. Reality would have won out. Death is not so easily defeated. It always gets its way.

Yet a few weeks later these followers of Jesus were proclaiming audaciously that Jesus was alive again—not as a resuscitated corpse, which would have only put off the inevitable, but as a resurrected being who would never die again. They even claimed that they had seen Jesus, talked to him, and touched him. They stated adamantly that Jesus had died, spent three days in a tomb, and then been resurrected. So sure were they of their experience that the apostles preached it everywhere, were martyred because they would not deny it, and lived with a joy, hope, and purpose that few in history have ever achieved. There is no record that any of them broke rank, disclaiming their story and admitting that they had invented it because they did not want to accept Jesus' death. There is no question that Jesus' disciples firmly believed what they proclaimed.

It is possible to explain their faith as mass delusion or hallucination or deception. But those explanations are more fanciful than the disciples' own rather simple and straightforward claim that Jesus had been killed, had somehow absorbed sin, evil, and death into himself, and had been raised from the grave. The resurrection was his vindication. Death does not have the final word; life does. Jesus' death and resurrection made it possible. He now has the authority and desire to give life to those who want and need it. Though the experience of death is universal, the experience of a resurrection is not. What made the disciples so different from the rest of us who have experienced catastrophic loss is not the terrible experience of loss itself, but their experience of Jesus' resurrection.

In his earthly ministry Jesus performed signs and wonders as signs of God's presence on earth. The deaf were made to hear, the blind to see, the lame to walk, and the dead to live again. But sooner or later those who had their hearing restored went deaf again—if not before death, then obviously in death. Those who were given sight went blind again, those who were made to walk went lame again, and those who were given life died again. Suffering and death won out in the end. In other words, Jesus' miracles were not the ultimate reason for his coming. His great victory was not his miracles but his resurrection. The grave could not hold him, so perfect was his life, so perfectly sacrificial his death. Jesus conquered death and was raised by God to a life that would never die again. The Easter story tells us that the last chapter of the human story is not death but life. Jesus' resurrection guarantees it. All tears and pain and sorrow will be swallowed up in everlasting life and pure, inextinguishable joy.

Of course that is in the future. But we live in the present, which is often full of sorrow and pain. Suffering engenders a certain degree of ambivalence in those of us who believe in the resurrection. We feel the pain of our present circumstances, which reminds us of what we have lost; yet we hope for future release and victory. We doubt, yet try to believe; we suffer, yet long for real healing; we inch hesitantly toward death, yet see death as the door to resurrection. This ambivalence of the soul reveals the dual nature of life. We are creatures made of dust; yet we know we were made for something more. A sense of eternity resides in our hearts. Living with this ambivalence is both difficult and vital. It stretches our souls, challenging us to acknowledge our mortality and yet to continue to hope for final victory—the victory Jesus won for us in his death and resurrection, a victory that awaits us only on the other side of the grave.

That ambivalence is a regular feature of my life now. I feel both sadness and hope. Lately my son David has begun once again to struggle to make peace with the loss of his mother. He told me recently that he feels a kind of sadness all the time and does not even want to be happy in the same way he was before she died. In his mind it would be almost sacrilegious for him to be happy again. The other night we observed the third-year anniversary of the accident. During dinner David said, "Dad, if I had only gone to the bathroom after the powwow, Mom would still be alive. If you had been busier that day, Mom would still be alive." He does not want it to be true. Sometimes I worry about him—about all of them really. Sometimes I even worry about me. Then I sink into a sadness that makes me think we will never experience life again. My despondent mood casts a shadow over everything, even over my faith. On those occasions I find it hard to believe anything at all.

But then I gain perspective. I remind myself that suffering is not unique to us. It is the destiny of humanity. If this world were the only one there is, then suffering has the final say and all of us are a sorry lot. But generations of faithful Christians have gone before and will come after, and they have believed or will believe what I believe in the depths of my soul. Jesus is at the center of it all. He defeated sin and death through his crucifixion and resurrection. Then light gradually dawns once again in my heart, and hope returns. I find reason and courage to keep going and to continue believing. Once again my soul increases its capacity for hope as well as for sadness. I end up believing with greater depth and joy than I had before, even in my sorrow.

A Community of Brokenness

I did not weep for the six million Jews or the two million Poles or the one million Serbs or the five million Russians—I was unprepared to weep for all humanity—but I did weep for these others who in one way or another had become dear to me.

William Styron

Loss is a universal experience. Like physical pain, we know it is real because sooner or later all of us experience it. But loss is also a solitary experience. Again, like physical pain, we know it is real only because we experience it uniquely within ourselves. When a person says, "You just don't know what I have gone through and how much I have suffered," we must acknowledge that he or she is entirely correct. We do not know and cannot know.

But then again, that person will never know what we have gone through and how much we have suffered either. Each person's experience is his or her own, even if, on the face of it, the experience appears similar to many others. Though suffering itself is universal, each experience of suffering is unique because each person who goes through it is unique. Who the self was before the loss, what the self feels in the loss, and how the self responds to the loss makes each person's experience different from all others. That is why suffering loss is a solitary experience. That is also why each of us must ultimately face it alone. No one can deliver us, substitute for us, or mitigate the pain in us.

But loss does not have to isolate us or make us feel lonely. Though it is a solitary experience we must face alone, loss is also a common experience that can lead us to community. It can create a community of brokenness. We must enter the darkness of loss alone, but once there we will find others with whom we can share life together.

By the time I arrived at the hospital, close friends were already there waiting for me. Within the next twenty-four hours other friends from around the country came to grieve the loss with me and my family. I was overwhelmed by the support. Since then I have talked with many of them about the experience, especially about their initial reaction to the tragedy. A couple who came from

Chicago told me recently about the feeling of utter devastation and inadequacy that swept over them when I called to tell them about the accident. When Steve and Kathy arrived at my home after their flight from Chicago, they glanced at each other before getting out of the car. The meeting of their weary eyes said it all in a language too deep for words. Questions confused them; answers eluded them. They decided in that moment simply to be present with me in spite of their helplessness and brokenness. Throwing caution to the wind, they walked into the house and embraced me in tears, though they had no idea what to say to comfort me and the children. They chose to make themselves available, vulnerable, and present to our suffering. They became a part of our community of brokenness.

Yet community does not result automatically from the experience of loss, for at least two reasons. First, public and tragic losses, like mine, always engender a groundswell of support that ends almost as quickly as it begins. We should not necessarily fault friends for the brevity or superficiality of their support. I have been prone to do the same myself. On many occasions I have sent a note to someone who suffered loss, visited that person once or twice, prayed sporadically over the course of a few weeks or months, and then have largely forgotten about it. I wanted to express concern, which I did. But I did not choose to embrace the suffering and did not allow it to change my life. In most cases I lacked the time and energy; in a few cases I also lacked the willingness and heart. In any case, I kept a safe distance and avoided the inconvenience of making the sacrifices that suffering people really need. Like most people, I did not want to expose myself to pain because it threatened to undermine my quest for happiness.

Sometimes such distance is inevitable and even healthy. I received dozens of meals, hundreds of phone calls, and thousands of cards and letters in the weeks following the accident. These gestures of support and sympathy meant a great deal to our whole family. The sheer volume showed how much people cared. Still, I did not have the time and energy to share myself with every one of these concerned friends. I did not have enough room in my soul to let all of them in. I could not keep retelling the same story, update people on what was happening to my children, or explain what I was thinking and how I was feeling during the many bleak days and months following the accident. The vast majority of those who genuinely grieved for us and with us had to return to their routine lives, for my sake as much as for theirs. I had to limit the number of visitors and put a stop to the help that was offered. On one occasion I actually took time during an adult Sunday school class I was teaching at our church to tell friends and supporters how my family and I were managing the trauma and making sense of the tragedy. They wanted to know, and they deserved to know; but I could not talk to each of them individually. It was natural, therefore, that a winnowing effect drastically decreased the number of people who functioned as my intimate community.

The second reason why community does not result automatically from suffering has to do with the private and sometimes shameful nature of many losses. My loss was overwhelmingly public, and the response was overwhelmingly sympathetic. That often happens in the case of tragedies like the one I faced. But some kinds of losses, like sexual abuse and infertility, are usually private. Most people never hear about them or, if they do, hear only enough to respond ineptly to the peculiar signs of behavior that may surface. Instead of becoming a community of support for these wounded people, they may actually prolong and aggravate the suffering because of their ignorance or insensitivity, which may be due to no fault of their own.

I can still hear the advice that was given to Lynda during the many years we struggled with infertility. Though intended to be helpful, it usually ended up being hurtful. "Just relax, then you'll get pregnant." "The Lord is just saving the blessing for you until you're ready for it." "Have you tried the technique of . . . ?" "The longer you wait, the more precious your baby will be to you." These words of advice put Lynda off. She wanted people to listen with sensitivity or, better yet, to mind their own business. Trite answers were a poor replacement for compassion. Perhaps these friends believed their own advice, as if it embodied ancient wisdom handed down faithfully from one generation to the next. Or perhaps they blabbered advice they did not even believe themselves because they could not tolerate Lynda's painful silence and felt an obligation to say something to make her feel better. They assumed that words, however lame, would do the trick. They made noise, but silence would have been more helpful and wise.

Other kinds of losses, like divorce, terminal illness, disability, and chronic unemployment, often contain unpleasant aspects that alienate or offend people who become more judgmental than sympathetic and more frightened than understanding. Divorce, for example, often forces people to take sides. It divides communities, alienates friends, and infuriates potential supporters who grow weary of the conflicts and become disillusioned when two adults do not seem able or willing to settle their differences. The people who do remain loyal are often the least likely to exercise discernment and provide the wise counsel a divorced person needs. Instead, they reinforce their friend's intransigence, agree with their complaints, and applaud their independence and willfulness.

Likewise, losses like terminal illness, AIDS, and disability often terrify. People wonder if they will catch some exotic disease.

They recoil in the presence of someone who has lost hair, weight, beauty, or physique. They feel uncomfortable in hospitals and squirm at silence because they do not know what to say. So they remain distant, wanting to help but fearing vulnerability. They are put off by the illness or disability and are threatened by the ominous reminder that it could happen to them just as easily. Or they avoid the pain of others because it threatens to dismantle their well-built defenses against their own losses. They become protective of the self that resists facing mortality.

My first encounter with death as a young pastor reminds me of how easy it is to recoil from the smell and ugliness of people who are wasting away. When I first saw the old man in bed, I remember thinking to myself, "God, he looks terrible! What am I doing here?" I prayed for him and then bolted from the room as fast as I could. I felt uncomfortable in his presence. His was an alien and threatening world to me. Death was too close, too palpable, too odious—a silent and ominous visitor in the room. I wanted desperately to escape it, for it was suffocating me with its oppressive presence.

I mentioned my friend Steve, who became a quadriplegic, in a previous chapter. Steve told me that after his accident most of his friends gradually faded away, for a variety of reasons. Some did not want to make the time and expend the effort to be with him. Others felt uncomfortable and inadequate around him. Either they did not know what to say, or they recoiled from the implicit threat that his disability represented. If it could happen to him, it could happen to them too. The immobile body lying in front of them was not the Steve they once knew or wanted to know. They did not want to visit if their old friend was gone. Steve therefore lost his community after the accident, except for one cousin, who has remained faithful to this day.

Community does not simply happen spontaneously, except in rare occurrences when conditions are right. Not even the unique circumstances of catastrophic loss are sufficient to create community. When people suffering loss do find community, it comes as a result of conscious choices they and other people make.

First of all, it requires a choice on the part of those who want to provide community for suffering friends. They must be willing to be changed by someone else's loss, though they might not have been directly affected by it. Good comfort requires empathy, forces adjustments, and sometimes mandates huge sacrifices. Comforters must be prepared to let the pain of another become their own and so let it transform them. They will never be the same after that decision. Their own world will be permanently altered by the presence of one who suffers. It will bring an end to detachment, control, and convenience. It will prevent them from ever thinking again that the world is a safe place full of nice people, positive experiences, and favorable circumstances.

Time and again I have heard the same comment from my closest friends. "You have no idea, Jerry, how much your experience has changed us." They have mentioned the impact of the tragedy on their relationships and priorities and quest for meaning. They are changed because they chose to get involved and to allow my suffering to become theirs. They refused to give me only a month or a year to return to life as it was for me before the loss. Since they knew life would not be the same for me, they decided that it would not be the same for them either.

John was barely two when the accident occurred. Suddenly he had a broken femur, a dead mother, and a distressed father. His world was thrown into chaos, as if he had been dropped into a whirlpool. Close friends from the college, Ron and Julie, visited me at the hospital every day. They asked me one day if I had any idea who would provide care for John when I was working. Before I could answer, Julie offered to be John's surrogate mother "for the long haul," as she put it. I resisted the idea at first. But she met every one of my questions with a cogent answer and a mother's resolve. So for three years now Julie has provided daytime child care for John, and Ron has helped as well. Julie has attended some of his preschool functions. She has taken John to the doctor's office when I was not able to. She has integrated him into her family and given him special attention. Yet she has not insisted on being called "mother" but has preserved and honored John's memory of his own mother. The impact of her sacrificial service for John and me has been incalculable. I believe that John's happy disposition and security is largely the result of the huge investment she has made in him.

A small group of men from the college and community decided to meet weekly with me after the accident to give me support, and I frequently saw them at other times during the week as well. We have met together for three years now, and the group has long since moved beyond concentrating exclusively on my needs as a grieving widower. My colleagues in the department in which I teach have enveloped me with loving concern, and we remain, to this day, the closest group of people I have ever worked with professionally. Other colleagues at the college have encouraged me to pursue my professional aspirations, in spite of the limited hours for work I have at my disposal. Friends in the community have welcomed me into the same social circle to which I belonged while I was married.

Above all, my sister and brother-in-law, Diane and Jack, who have been my best friends for years, have helped me adjust to life as a single parent, establish new patterns in my home, and set a course for the future. We spent hundreds of hours on the phone together that first year, and we still talk two or three times a week. They have given me invaluable advice about raising my children, and they have suggested creative ways to manage my home more efficiently. They have also reflected on the tragedy with me to probe it for meaning and to understand the loss in the light of our faith. Many of the ideas appearing in this book were first discussed with them.

I have also experienced the church at its best. I was a member of First Presbyterian Church when the accident occurred. Members of the church immediately rallied to my side. In the short run they overwhelmed our family with food and attention, and in the long run they joined me in grieving our loss. But not ours alone. My tragedy was so public that it gave many people in the congregation permission to face their own losses, some of which had been buried or ignored for years. I have observed churches fail, as many people have. Many churches are full of hypocrites, bigots, and lukewarm Christians, which should surprise no one. Still, I found my church community sympathetic and loyal. I risked giving the church a chance, and the church came through for me and my family.

The communities to which I belonged before the accident, in other words, were the communities to which I belonged after the accident. They supported me as I mourned, adjusted, and changed. Their commitment to remain loyal kept me from having to make still another adjustment—to form a new circle of friends. Their faithfulness created the stability and continuity of relationships I needed to enter the darkness and find a new life after the loss. I grieved *with* these friends. I grieved *because of* these friends, for their presence in my life reminded me of the past I had lost. But I also grew because these friends provided security and familiarity in a world that had fallen apart. They made life both worse and better for me, a reminder of what it used to be and a challenge to discover what it could be after the accident.

Living in the same house had a similar impact. At first it was not easy living in such familiar territory, sleeping in the same bed, and looking at the hundreds of objects—pictures, albums, decorations, books, posters, and all the rest—that awakened memories of life before the accident. Our entire home reminded me of Lynda and Diana Jane's absence. I felt torment every time I walked in the door, as if I was a starving man who smelled a favorite food he could not eat. But it also provided a familiar setting in which the children and I could establish a new identity as a family of four. Our home became a laboratory of experimentation and discovery. It made us mourn; it also helped us to grow.

A little over a year after the accident I decided to stay home for the Thanksgiving weekend rather than visit family on the other side of the state. The winter started early that year, which made us virtually homebound. I was also enduring a massive depression, into which I had plunged at the first anniversary of the accident. That depression only exacerbated the feeling of emptiness and isolation I felt during those four days at home, which seemed to stretch into years. Yet the four of us had a wonderful time together. We felt comfortable being a family of four, celebrating a holiday together. We ate well and played hard. Even so, that long weekend bore down on me like a tree that had fallen across my chest. Sometimes I could hardly breathe, I felt so oppressed by the sadness. Yet it also gave me confidence that we could do well together, even during holidays. It was the hardest holiday I have yet faced; it was the most liberating too.

The experience of community has taught me another lesson as well. Not only must people who want to comfort someone in pain make a decision to do so, but people who need the comfort must also decide to receive it. Their responsibility will include facing the darkness with courage, learning new skills, and striving for mutuality in friendships. In other words, they must take command of their lives as much as they are able to, in spite of their distress and brokenness. I learned this lesson largely through the gentle encouragement of friends, who urged me to make wise choices in my loss. For example, Ron, Julie, and I drew clear boundaries to protect me from taking advantage of them and to protect them from feeling resentment toward me. Julie and I worked out a schedule for caregiving, and I hired Monica to be a part-time nanny. One of Monica's duties was to watch Julie's youngest child while she worked swing shift as a registered nurse and Ron worked at the college.

A good friend, Susan, volunteered to drive Catherine and David to and from school, and she has continued doing that valuable service for three years. But I worked myself into the rotation of carpooling as quickly as I could and, over the past three years, have coached her son in soccer. My desire to assume as much responsibility as I could forced me to develop important management skills and to budget my time wisely so that my home would run smoothly.

Of course it has not always done so. I have served my share of overcooked chicken dinners, missed a few rehearsals, showed up late for practices, and neglected to send a snack to school. On one occasion I was teaching a class of fifty college students when I suddenly remembered I had forgotten to pick Catherine up at school for an important concert. It would have been less awkward had we only planned to attend the concert. But Catherine was scheduled to perform in it as only one of three girls singing first soprano, which meant that her absence would be obvious to all, especially to the director. I rushed out of class in a panic and called her school. But it was too late by then. We missed the entire event. Of course I apologized to the director later, but the apology was scant help to those who had to perform without Catherine.

I realized soon after the accident that I had another significant responsibility to fulfill too, and that concerned my role in the community as an interpreter of my experience. Friends wanted to listen and empathize; but they also wanted to learn, to reflect on the universal nature of suffering, and to make meaning for their own lives. So we became a reflective community together. I have told these friends many times how thankful I am for their sympathetic concern, and they have told me how grateful they are for the opportunity to find meaning for their lives in my experience of suffering. They were thus willing to be changed; I was willing to exercise responsibility. They never felt manipulated and used; I never felt patronized and pressured. The result was a *mutuality* in our relationships. All of us contributed, and all of us gained.

The result was love. We learned to love more deeply. That was especially, though not exclusively, true for me. I hesitated at first to risk loving again. There was a protective reflex in me that made me want to turn my back on everyone, even my own family. My experience taught me that loss reduces people to a state of almost total brokenness and vulnerability. I did not simply feel raw pain; I *was* raw pain. Consequently, I usually found myself on the receiving end of love and friendship. Eventually I had to decide, however, to become a contributing member of the community once again, not only willing to receive but also to give love.

That decision was not easy to make. It never is. It is natural that people feel cautious about loving again because they are afraid of losing again. Who in his or her right mind would ever want to feel such pain more than once? Is love worth it if it is that risky? Is it even possible to love after loss, knowing that other losses will follow? I have thought many times how devastating it would be for me if I lost another of my children, especially now that I have invested so much of myself into them. I am terrified by that possibility. Yet I cannot imagine not loving them either, which is even more abhorrent to me than losing them.

The risk of further loss, therefore, poses a dilemma. The problem of choosing *to love again* is that the choice to love means living under the constant threat of further loss. But the problem of choosing *not to love* is that the choice to turn from love means imperiling the life of the soul, for the soul thrives in an environment of love. Soul-full people love; soul-less people do not. If people want their souls to grow through loss, whatever the loss is, they must eventually decide to love even more deeply than they did before. They must respond to the loss by embracing love with renewed energy and commitment.

That was the choice I had to make, at any rate. Such a choice applied most immediately to my children, who desperately needed a parent who would love them through the tragedy. I came to see shortly after the accident that how my children would someday view and respond to the tragedy depended in part on how I cared for them as their father. About six months after the accident I received an unusual telephone call from a stranger who wanted to talk with me about her mother's death. It was the only conversation we ever had. I do not even remember her name. She said that her mother had died when she was ten years old. At the age of twenty she began to see a therapist, whom she saw on and off for six years. My first reaction to this information was anger and fear. I wondered why she had called if the only news she could give me was so bleak. But then she explained why she had gone to a therapist. It was not, as I had assumed, to address the loss of her mother. It was to deal with the loss of *her father*, who was still alive. Her father, she said, had responded to his wife's death by withdrawing from his children. Though they continued to live in the same household, he became emotionally distant and inaccessible. It was *his* response to the loss that became the most devastating loss to her, because she lost someone who was still alive and could have loved her but chose not to.

That phone call was a pure gift to me. It reminded me of the opportunity and privilege I had to be a father to three traumatized and bewildered children. I did not want one loss—the death of a mother—to lead to another, equally unbearable loss—the death of a father who was still alive. Enough destruction had occurred as it was. I was not willing to add to it by withdrawing from them and depriving them of the love they needed. I wanted to overcome evil by doing good.

Still, I realized then, as I do now, that there is an ominous dimension to love, especially after loss. If loss increases our capacity for love, then an increased capacity for love will only make us feel greater sorrow when suffering strikes again. There is no simple solution to this dilemma. Choosing to withdraw from people and to protect the self diminishes the soul; choosing to love even more deeply than before ensures that we will suffer again, for the choice to love requires the courage to grieve. We know that loss is not a once-in-a-lifetime experience. So naturally we dread the losses that loom ahead. But the greater loss is not suffering another loss itself but refusing to love again, for that may lead to the death of the soul.

It takes tremendous courage to love when we are broken. Yet I wonder if love becomes more authentic when it grows out of brokenness. Brokenness forces us to find a source of love outside ourselves. That source is God, whose essential nature is love. It seems paradoxical to put brokenness and love together, but I believe they belong together.

I have had wonderful encounters with people over these last three years. These were most meaningful when they came out of the common experience of suffering. A friend from the college watched helplessly as his wife endured a year's worth of treatment for breast cancer. My tragedy and his concern for his wife caused us to forge a deep friendship. An employee at the college has only recently been diagnosed with cancer. Once again, our conversations have struck deep chords in both of us. Recently I talked with a woman from our church who has AIDS, which she contracted from a bad blood transfusion. She has young children and fears for them; she loves her husband and feels for him. We discussed the peculiar nature of our circumstances. We probed for meaning, trying to make sense of it all. It was moving for me to hear her story and to share my own.

My appreciation for people has grown immeasurably since the accident, though I have never felt more fragile and inadequate. My loss joined brokenness and love together. Brokenness drove me to love, and I found a source of love that I could not find in myself. I found it in community, and in the God who creates and sustains community for broken people like me.

The Cloud of Witnesses

Galaxies revolve and dinosaurs breed and rain falls and people fall in love and uncles smoke cheap cigars and people lose their jobs and we all die—all for our good, the finished product, God's work of art, the kingdom of heaven. There's nothing outside heaven except hell. Earth is not outside heaven; it is heaven's workshop, heaven's womb.

PETER KREEFT

Lynda loved the music of J. S. Bach, and she played recordings of his organ music and choral works often. It was not simply the music, but also Bach's reason for writing it that moved her. Whenever he finished a composition, he signed it, "To the glory of God." Bach drew his inspiration from his Christian faith and from the Bible. Many of his choral works were based on biblical texts and were written for the church. He witnessed to his faith through the music he wrote. His music has borne witness to me over these past three years of the truth of the faith for which Bach lived and for which I seek now to live.

The Bible tells the stories of the great "cloud of witnesses,"[1] some of whom endured losses similar to the ones we face today and who have gone to the grave before us. They trusted God in their afflictions, loved him with their whole being, and obeyed him, even when obedience required sacrifice and led to death. This cast of characters—among them Job and Joseph, whom I have already mentioned—have helped me to believe. Their examples have kept me going, their songs have touched emotions in me that needed recognition and attention, their poetry has given me a language to express my complaints, pain, and hope, and their convictions have helped me decide what matters most in life. Their stories have provided me with perspective. I am not sure what I would have done or how I would have fared without the stories of these people who struggled and triumphed, just as I now struggle and hope to triumph. Because of them I see that I am only one of millions of people who in suffering believe nevertheless that God is still God.

This great cloud of witnesses includes more than the characters of the Bible, though these biblical characters obviously play the key role in showing us who God is and how God can be trusted, even in suffering. I have drawn inspiration over these past years from a variety of people and stories, and so have my children.

Music has soothed my soul. I have attended performances of Bach's *St. Matthew's Passion* and his *B Minor Mass* since the accident. These performances reminded me of the power that music has to touch the deepest places of the human heart. I discovered Gabriel Faure's *Requiem* several months after the accident. A requiem is a mass for the dead, and the text pleads for God to grant departed souls "eternal rest" and deliverance from "everlasting death." Faure's *Requiem* includes a final section describing a paradise that, by virtue of the sublimity of the music, I long to enter. In the months after the accident I listened almost every night to music like Faure's and Bach's, often into the early morning hours. Such music touched the anguish of my soul and gave me peace.

Poets have provided me with metaphors and images by which to understand and express my sorrow. A student gave me a copy of a poem written by a Puritan after one of his children died. The words this poet used to describe his sadness helped me voice my own. A colleague sent me a copy of William Blake's "Can I See Another's Woe," which explores the human experience of suffering in light of God's suffering.

Can I see another's woe, and not be in sorrow, too?
Can I see another's grief, and not seek for kind relief?
Can I see a falling tear, and not feel my sorrow's share?
Can a father see his child weep, nor be with sorrow filled?
Can a mother sit and hear an infant groan, an infant fear?

No, no! Never can it be! Never, never can it be!

And can he who smiles on all hear the wren with sorrows small,
Hear the small bird's grief and care, hear the woes
that infants bear,
And not sit beside the nest, pouring pity in their breast;

And not sit the cradle near, weeping tear on infant's tear;
And not sit both night and day wiping all our tears away?

O no! Never can it be! Never, never can it be!

He doth give His joy to all; He becomes an infant small,
He becomes a man of woe; He doth feel the sorrow, too.
Think not thou canst sigh a sigh, and thy Maker is not by;
Think not thou canst weep a tear, and thy Maker is not near,
O! He gives to us His joy that our grief He may destroy;
Till our grief is fled and gone, He doth sit by us and moan.

I read books and diaries that examined the relationship between faith and suffering. Writing in his journal after his wife's death, Thomas Shepherd captured the ambivalence I was feeling at the time, though he wrote these reflections more than three hundred years ago. In one paragraph Shepherd stated what his faith required him to believe—that life on earth is transitory and full of sorrow and that true life awaits the faithful in heaven. He recognized that sometimes saints suffer because they need God's discipline and grace. In the end, however, he concluded, "I am the Lord's, and he may do with me what he will. He did teach me to prize a little grace gained by a cross as a sufficient recompense for all outward losses." But then in the next paragraph he described with deep affection and longing the excellent qualities his wife possessed and the beautiful life they shared together. Her death was devastating to him because she was such a superior woman.

> But this loss was very great. She was a woman of incomparable meekness of spirit, toward myself especially, and very loving, of great prudence to take care for and order my family affairs, being neither too lavish nor sordid in anything, so that I knew not what was under her hands. . . . She

> had a spirit of prayer beyond ordinary of her time and experience. She was fit to die long before she did die. . . .

Shepherd affirmed the sovereignty of God and the promise of heaven, but he also mourned the loss of the good life he had on earth. His journal reflects what another Puritan wrote after the death of a loved one, "Now life will be a little less sweet, death a little less bitter."

This cloud of witnesses includes people from other cultures who have continued to believe in spite of, or perhaps because of, their suffering. I have read stories about courageous Roman Catholics in Latin America who resisted oppression and paid for it with their lives. I met a woman from China who was sentenced to work on a collective farm for many years because she was a Christian. Just today I attended a committee meeting to which one of the members, Jenny, brought along a two-year-old boy from Columbia who will be living with her family for eight months under the sponsorship of the Heal the Children program. He was brought to the United States to receive medical care to correct his multiple birth defects. So Jenny and her family are sharing in his suffering. These and many other saints belong to that same cloud of witnesses. They have faced circumstances far more torturous than mine and yet have endured and prevailed. They remind me every day that I am not alone but am a member of a vast community of suffering people that transcends my own space and time. I am grateful that I can keep their company and learn from them.

These people challenge me to believe and inspire me to serve a world that languishes under such misery. It is not surprising that loss often inspires people to sacrifice themselves for some greater purpose. They know how painful loss is. When they see other people suffer, they act out of compassion to alleviate their pain and work for change. The founder of MADD (Mothers Against Drunk Drivers) lost a child in an accident caused by a drunken driver. The founder of Prison Fellowship, an organization that serves prison inmates and their families, spent time in prison. The people who led the movement to build the Vietnam War Memorial in Washington, D.C., were themselves veterans or relatives of soldiers who died in combat. Some of the best therapists I know came from dysfunctional homes. Often the most helpful people have endured suffering themselves and turned their pain into a motivation to serve others.

My children have found a similar cloud of witnesses to help them grieve and to give them hope. A student on campus met with Catherine after the accident to tell about the loss of her own mother when she was Catherine's age. Other people—some complete strangers—wrote letters to tell us their own stories of loss and growth. The children read books and watched movies that somehow touched on the theme of loss. John asked me to read *Bambi* dozens of times after the accident. He made me pause every time we came to the section that told the story of the death of Bambi's mother. Sometimes he said nothing, and the two of us sat in a sad silence. Sometimes he cried. He talked about the similarity between Bambi's story and his own. "Bambi lost his mommy too," he said on several occasions. Then he added, "And Bambi became the Prince of the Forest." David showed interest in the biblical story of Joseph. Catherine found comfort in Disney's movie version of *Beauty and the Beast* because the main character, Belle, grew up without a mother and, as Catherine has observed, became an independent, intelligent, beautiful person.

This cloud of witnesses includes men and women out of the pages of Scripture, heroes from history, poets, storytellers, composers, and people from around the world, all of whom show us that we have not suffered alone nor in vain. They remind us that life is bigger than loss because God is bigger than loss. They bear witness to the truth that pain and death do not have the final word; God does.

That final word involves more than life on earth; it involves life in heaven as well, the final destination of this great cloud of witnesses. I find myself thinking often about heaven. Life on earth is real and good. I once enjoyed it with the loved ones whom I lost, and I still enjoy it without them. But life here is not the end. Reality is more than we think it to be. There is another and greater reality that envelops this earthly one. Earth is not outside heaven, as the philosopher Peter Kreeft wrote; it is heaven's workshop, heaven's womb. My loved ones have entered that heaven and have joined those who died before them. They are in heaven now because they believed in Jesus, who suffered, died, and was raised for their sake. They live in the presence of God and in a reality I long to enter, but only in God's good time.

The book of Revelation describes a scene from the future in which Jesus himself embraces and restores all those who have suffered and died. He wipes away their tears and heals their brokenness. Then he welcomes them into the bliss and splendor and peace of his eternal kingdom.[2] That scene reminds me that heaven is our true destiny, however good life on earth seems to be. Heaven is our real home, where we have always longed to be.

Heritage in a Graveyard

History is one tapestry. No eye can venture to compass more than a hand's-breadth. . . . There is no happiness equal to that of being aware that one has a part in a design.

THORTON WILDER

I take my children to visit the graveyard whenever we travel to Lynden, where Lynda, Diana Jane, and my mother are buried. I think they like these visits. We talk together about the people who died, reflect on the accident and what has happened since, and discuss how different life would have been if they had not died. Sometimes my children say they wish that they had died in the accident, too, which seems normal and understandable to me, since I think the same thing myself. We also stroll through the graveyard and read gravestones. I tell them stories about the people I know who are buried there, and together we imagine what life was like for them, how they lived and died, and who was left behind to mourn after they were gone. These occasions at the graveyard give us a sense of heritage.

Heritage has always been important to me, but never more than in the last three years. Much of who I am is a product of the heritage given me at my birth. My story is part of a much larger story that I did not choose. I was assigned a role for which I did not audition. Yet I have the power to choose how I will live out that story and play that role. I want to live my story well and play my role with as much integrity and joy as I can.

Both my mother and mother-in-law lost their mothers when they were little girls. My children, therefore, have to endure now what their grandmothers had to endure so many years ago when they lost their mothers, and I face the same challenges that my grandfathers faced two generations ago when they became widowers. I have thought often about what my two grandfathers did after their wives died at such a young age. Those two men were thrust into a set of circumstances that must have devastated them and pushed them to the limit. I have wondered how they coped with the stress, sorrow, and responsibilities. They had to live out stories that they did not choose. It became their destiny.

Now I have my own story to live out, my own destiny to fulfill. Someday my story is going to be the heritage that others will inherit and talk about when they stroll through a graveyard and read my name and dates on the gravestone. I have gained much from my heritage and community; now I feel resolved to give much. I want to preserve the heritage my mother introduced to me, to strengthen that heritage if I can, and to pass on a tradition of faith and virtue that future generations will want and need. I want to honor the dead who have gone before me and bless the living who will come after me. Whether and to what extent I succeed will depend on the choices I make and the grace I receive.

My children still feel sorrow, as I expect they will for the rest of their lives. The other day David came upstairs at midnight looking for me. He was crying hard. He crawled on my lap and sat there for awhile. Then he expressed a great longing for his mother. Catherine asked me recently how she could "become a woman without Mom." John still pulls his picture album down from the bookshelf and looks at his baby and toddler pictures. He often says wistfully, "I miss Mommy." These expressions of sadness surface regularly in our home. They are as natural as noise, fun, and fights. Loss is a part of who we are as a family.

The consequences of tragedy never really end, not after two years or ten years or a hundred years. My cousin Leanna has just undergone a stem cell transplant as a severe measure to combat the multiple myeloma. It is another reminder of the irreversible course down which her life is leading. She hopes and prays for healing, as her whole family does, but she also mourns when she considers the difficulty of the past three years and the uncertainty of the future. I recently received a letter from Andy and Mary, who updated me on the progress of Sarah. Their letter was filled with hope and gratitude. Yet there was an undeniable tone of realism in it, too. Sarah's presence in their home has altered the course of their lives permanently, and they are well aware of the problems that lie ahead. They feel the effects of their loss whenever they hear Sarah cry, take her to the doctor, pay medical bills, or plan for the future. I also heard from Steve, who spoke with gratitude about the stable condition of his health, which is allowing him to spend much of his waking hours in a wheelchair rather than in bed. He is making the most of the time, expanding his printing business and working at his computer. But he knows that these stretches of relief from bedsores, kidney stones, and other health problems are fleeting. Steve will be a quadriplegic until the day he dies, unless God acts to heal him. Every day he must face the grim reminders of his loss.

Likewise, I will bear the mark of the tragedy for the rest of my life, though it will fade over time. Even if I remarry and adopt children, I will feel the loss till I die. I will be forever discovering and experiencing new dimensions of the tragedy. The loss will continue to influence my life. I can only hope it will be for the better.

Not surprisingly, then, I still feel sorrow. I look with longing at pictures, think often about the relationships I wish I had with each of my lost family members, and feel their absence every day, especially at important events like soccer matches, music recitals, holidays, vacations, and birthdays. The passage of time has mitigated the feeling of pain, panic, and chaos. But it has also increased my awareness of how complex and far-reaching the loss has been. I am still not "over" it; I have still not "recovered." I still wish my life were different and they were alive. But I have changed and grown.

I also feel the emptiness that comes after having faced a challenge or danger that is now apparently past. I have heard of Vietnam veterans who felt a profound letdown after returning home. They missed the keen concentration that was required of them to survive in combat. Though the war was horrible to them, it nevertheless forced them to use their senses and energy in a way that made them feel intensely alive. Likewise, I worked long and hard to survive loss, and I now feel less energetic and focused than I used to, although no less contented. I realize it is time to redirect some of my energy. Still, I strangely miss the awareness and vitality I felt when I had to invest so much of myself into facing the darkness, finding meaning in the loss, and affirming life in the midst of death.

The accident itself bewilders me as much today as it did three years ago. Much good has come from it, but all the good in the world will never make the accident itself good. It remains a horrible, tragic, and evil event to me. A million people could be helped as a result of the tragedy, but that would not be enough to explain and justify it. The badness of the event and the goodness of the results are related, to be sure, but they are not the same. The latter is a consequence of the former, but the latter does not make the former legitimate or right or good. I do not believe that I lost three members of my family *in order that* I might change for the better, raise three healthy children, or write a book. I still want them back, and I always will, no matter what happens as a result of their deaths.

Yet the grief I feel is sweet as well as bitter. I still have a sorrowful soul; yet I wake up every morning joyful, eager for what the new day will bring. Never have I felt as much pain as I have in the last three years; yet never have I experienced as much pleasure in simply being alive and living an ordinary life. Never have I felt so broken; yet never have I been so whole. Never have I been so aware of my weakness and vulnerability; yet never have I been so content and felt so strong. Never has my soul been more dead; yet never has my soul been more alive. What I once considered mutually exclusive—sorrow and joy, pain and pleasure, death and life—have become parts of a greater whole. My soul has been stretched.

Above all, I have become aware of the power of God's grace and my need for it. My soul has grown because it has been awakened to the goodness and love of God. God has been present in my life these past three years, even mysteriously in the accident. God will continue to be present to the end of my life and through all eternity. God is growing my soul, making it bigger, and filling it with himself. My life is being transformed. Though I have endured pain, I believe that the outcome is going to be wonderful.

Lynda, Diana Jane, and my mother Grace have gone to death before me. Someday I too will die, as will Catherine, David, and John. As long as I remain alive, I want to live as joyfully, serenely, and productively as I can. My heritage has set a standard for me, and I feel honored to uphold it.

The supreme challenge to anyone facing catastrophic loss involves facing the darkness of the loss on the one hand, and learning to live with renewed vitality and gratitude on the other. This challenge is met when we learn to take the loss into ourselves and to be enlarged by it, so that our capacity to live life well and to know God intimately increases. To escape the loss is far less healthy—and far less realistic, considering how devastating loss can be—than to grow from it. Loss can diminish us, but it can also expand us. It depends, once again, on the choices we make and the grace we receive. Loss can function as a catalyst to transform us. It can lead us to God, the only One who has the desire and power to give us life.

Lynda and I planned our wedding with a great deal of care. We paid more attention to the meaning of marriage than to the details of the wedding, and this fit Lynda's personality well, for she was always more interested in depth of ideas than in appearances. We chose to sing one hymn, "Be Thou My Vision." I chose that same hymn for the funeral. It captures what we believed when we were married, what I believe now, and what I will continue to believe until I go to the grave.

Be Thou my vision, O Lord of my heart;
Nought be all else to me, save that Thou art;
Thou my best thought, by day or by night,
Waking or sleeping, Thy presence my light.

Riches I heed not, nor vain, empty praise,
Thou mine inheritance, now and always;
Thou and Thou only, first in my heart,
Great God of heaven, my treasure Thou art.

Be Thou my wisdom, and Thou my true word;
I ever with Thee and Thou with me, Lord;
Heart of my own heart, whatever befall,
Still be my vision, O Ruler of all.

NOTES

Chapter 3: ***Darkness Closes In***

[1]Romans 8:26–27.

[2]Viktor Frankl, *Man's Search for Meaning*, 3d ed. (New York: Simon and Schuster, 1984), 80–81.

[3]Ibid., 74.

[4]Ibid., 76.

[5]Nicholas Wolterstorff, *Lament for a Son* (Grand Rapids: Eerdmans, 1987), 96–97.

Chapter 4: ***The Silent Scream of Pain***

[1]William Styron, *Darkness Visible: A Memoir of Madness* (New York: Random, 1990).

Chapter 5: ***Sailing on a Sea of Nothingness***

[1]Matthew 5:4.

[2]Mark 8:36.

Chapter 6: ***The Amputation of the Familiar Self***

[1]Philippians 3:13–14.

Chapter 7: ***A Sudden Halt to Business As Usual***

[1]Romans 8:39.

Chapter 8: *The Terror of Randomness*

[1]See the biblical book of Job.

[2]See Genesis 37–50.

[3]Genesis 50:20.

Chapter 14: *The Cloud of Witnesses*

[1]Hebrews 12:1.

[2]Revelation 21.

Notes

Notes

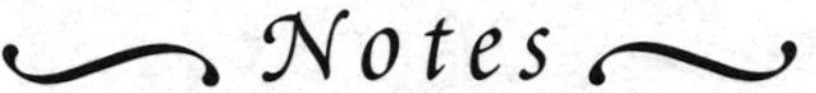

Notes

Notes

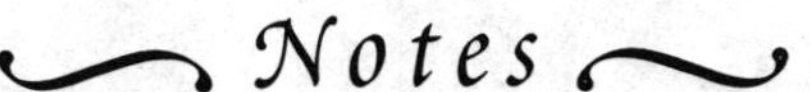
Notes

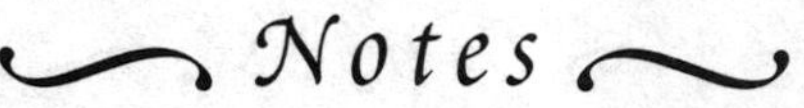
Notes